GETTING IT RIGHT!

Lessons on Insights-Driven Marketing Strategy

JONATHAN WEINER

Getting It Right!

Lessons on Insights-Driven Marketing Strategy

Copyright © Jonathan Weiner (2020)

ISBN: 978-1-950336-14-2

Published by

BestsellingBook.com

Table of Contents

Author's Note 5

Who Is This Book's Intended Audience? 9

It's a Good Day to Be Scared 11

Part 1: Product-Market Fit **15**

Chapter 1: Getting It Right – Overcoming a Nagging Problem 17

Chapter 2: I Love Market Research 33

Chapter 3: The Future Defines the Present 51

Chapter 4: Birds of a Feather 75

Chapter 5: The North Star 101

Chapter 6: Tactics in Search of a Strategy 133

Part 2: Execution **151**

Chapter 7: Integrated Marketing Is Marketing... and Vice Versa 153

Chapter 8: WYSIWYG 183

Chapter 9: Pricing 199

Chapter 10: It Works 215

Chapter 11: Developing a Brilliant Solution to a Nagging Problem 235

Bonus Chapter

Chapter 12: Profit with Honor 279

End Notes 293

Acknowledgments 301

Author's Bio 303

Table of Contents

Author's Note

The events portrayed in this book are composites of actual events. In most cases, the names of the participants in the stories have been intentionally excluded.

For the Guffizah

"*Sometimes you can get shown the light in the strangest of places if you look at it right.*"

—Robert Hunter

Who Is This Book's Intended Audience?

I wrote this book for anyone who is involved with marketing, innovation and growth. My goal is to encourage them and their colleagues to take the right and necessary steps to use foundational insights and insight-based frameworks to build marketing strategy.

This book lays out a sequential way to build marketing strategy— from understanding the power of insights to their applications in targeting, branding, strategy, and execution.

Marketers and non-marketers alike may have encountered some of this content, but not presented in this way or this order or with such a heavy focus on the benefits of foundational insights on strategy, brand-building, marketing, and innovation. Many in marketing leadership positions aren't marketers by training. This book is definitely for them.

I hope that CMOs will recognize the value of the processes in this book, and hand the book down to their team to use for their brands. One CMO can inspire a whole lot of people. Those people will move from job to job and company to company, and carry these techniques with them. The impact of this book could reach well beyond one organization to many.

For those in the start-up world—founders, venture capitalists, and private equity managers—you should find this book helpful for finding a quicker path to product-market fit.

And of course, this book is excellent for any young market researcher or business student as a guide on how to create insight-based marketing strategy.

It's a Good Day to Be Scared

I love to ski, and I love to watch ski movies. I've been skiing since I was a kid. But I only got really involved in it when my son Zach and I started skiing together every year at some new location around the planet.

As Zach grew, his appetite for more challenging terrain increased. And, with that, my parental responsibility of keeping him safe transformed into survival and keeping me safe! As "our" appetite for more challenging terrain increased, the slopes got steeper, and the diamonds turned blacker and increased in number.

One evening, we were watching a ski movie that had some of the best all-mountain skiers tackling crazy, jaw-dropping terrain. As they interviewed these daredevils, one of them said that every skier, even the best, is scared at the top of these slopes. And at some point in the movie, he said, as he looked out the window in the morning toward the mountains, the snow, and the blue sky, ready to embrace the day, "It's a good day to be scared."

About five years ago, Zach said I was getting old, and we should knock off Alaska Heli-skiing. A few months before we were about to go, I felt I might be skiing above my skill level. So, I found Kristen Ulmer, recognized as being one of the best big mountain extreme skiers in the world—known for big cliff jumps and "you fall, you die" descents. Kristen is also an author, and a specialist in helping people overcome their fears. So, Zach and I went off to Utah to take a lesson from Kristen essentially to allay my fears. Her guidance was just the kind of reassurance I needed right before heading to Alaska.

Over the day, we explored quite a few of Kristen's Zen techniques on how to approach fear. Then, after a long day of skiing and visualization, she said, "Everyone is scared at the top of the mountain. Be open, and you can do it."

Zach and me in the Chugach Mountains

What's That Have to Do with This Book?

This book is about taking smart and thoughtful approaches to marketing strategy and growth. The ideas in the book are based on my experiences with big and little brands, big budgets and small ones, advanced processes and simple ones. This stuff will work for all brands and in virtually every category. Like Kristen Ulmer reframed the way I approach skiing, I want to make you think about the way you approach marketing strategy.

To quote Neil deGrasse Tyson:

> *"The most important moments of your life aren't decided by what you know—they're decided by how you think."*

I want to share with you how I think, and hopefully, in turn, help shape the way you think.

Frameworks

There are yoga practices that link different postures together to achieve a specific outcome. They get a name to go with it. The postures have been available for hundreds of years—probably longer—but no one person owns these postures.

Similarly, the ideas and frameworks in this book, in some form, have been around in the collective marketing mindset for some time. I have drawn these together to achieve a specific outcome: fact-based, customer-first, insight-led marketing strategy. If I could brand it "JW's Wheel of Fortune," I would, but I'd be overreaching.

Not Another Marketing Book

The content in this book has been drawn from years of experience, and it can sometimes feel instructive. One friend warned me "not to write another book of 'Marketers marketing to Marketers.'"

Zach (a Googler) told me that I had to offer more of myself and my journey—to bring you, the reader, into my experiences. So, I have added personal moments that will set context for each chapter.

Embrace the Opportunity

I believe one of the principal reasons for failure in marketing and innovation is the reluctance to be open to the opinions and ideas of others. Listening to others requires curiosity, a willingness to listen, and the flexibility to stay open to what comes your way. That's what I'm asking of you as you turn to the next chapter. Keep an open mind. Embrace the opportunity to learn.

There is something a little scary about letting go and embracing a different approach. Imagine you're at the top of the mountain. Be open, you can do it.

It's a good day to be scared.

PART 1
Product-Market Fit

*Product/market fit, also known as **product-market fit**, is the degree to which a **product** satisfies a strong **market** demand. **Product/market fit** has been identified as a first step to building a successful venture.*
—**Wikipedia**[1]

"Anything worth doing is worth doing it right."

—Hunter S. Thompson

CHAPTER 1

Getting It Right – Overcoming a Nagging Problem

Marketing is a window into our culture. It reflects the thoughts, desires, and fears of customers across a broad spectrum of races, genders, ages, lifestyles, and geographies. It reflects all that matters to people, and in a way, to our society.

Many creative leaders, at their core, understand the psychosocial nature of customers and their needs. But CMOs today are also becoming increasingly more executional. Tenures are short, and demand generation has increasingly become the focus of the job. The challenges that face marketing professionals have branched off into a multitude of tangents. The creative piece is just one aspect. Marketers are planners, and managers of tactics—digital tactics, media plans, budgets, pricing, and the list goes on.

And, great creative is harder to acquire with tighter timelines and profit accountabilities. Agencies offer the outside chance that you will find the right creative, but there is the risk they can miss the mark and be disappointing. Also, not every business can afford a creative agency.

In my thirty-five-plus years, I have worked with a wide range of business leaders—and I've seen a wide range of problems across many categories. One thing I've felt is that time constraints always seems to get in the way of doing the right work.

As my college professor and colleague Kevin Clancy used to say, "There's never enough time or money to do it right the first time, but always enough time and money to fix it the second time."

Consider the adage, "Anything worth doing is worth doing it right."

Doing it right matters. Getting it right matters. It matters to the brand, the company, the shareholders, and most of all, to the customers. It should matter to you. What you do matters.

Dedicated, and talented marketers have a passion for "doing it right." They want to create great work, and create a moment for their brands.

What you will get from this book is solid and straightforward thinking for doing marketing strategy and branding properly, leveraging insights and frameworks.

By leaning on these approaches, you take away the worry about whether or not you're doing it right. Instead, trust them, and use them to create a space for you to tap into your creative side, meet the needs of your customer, make the time for outstanding work, and create those great moments for your brands.

Getting things right is not that hard. It just takes the will and the discipline to want to do it correctly. I encourage you to commit to the approach, to be focused on the customer, and to dedicate yourself to creating great work.

1. What Does Getting It Right Mean?

I grew up outside of Philadelphia as the son of a butcher who was the son of a butcher who was the son of a butcher.

Three Generations of Butchers
(I'm on the left; my brother is on the right)

The family store was in a large indoor farmers market with about twenty or so other stores inside. The market was in a poorer section of Delaware, and our customers were those mainly trying to make ends meet. While I was learning the trade, I spent years behind the counter, waiting on customers.

The Family Butcher Shop – Delaware Valley Meats

My grandfather, father, and I would drive the two hours back and forth, to and from Philadelphia, discussing the business. I was maybe fourteen years old. It seemed simple to me. I waited for the customer to tell me what they wanted, I would wrap it up, and they would pay for it. But if you watched my father and grandfather wait on customers, you'd see how they would talk to the customer, laugh with them, listen to their troubles, and usually, enjoy each interaction. My grandfather had the most infectious smile, one that made anyone he spent time with happy.

This was not about selling meat or putting food on the table. This was about developing an intimate understanding of the customer, asking them questions about what they needed, what the occasion was, how many they were feeding, whether they wanted more for next week, or if there was a dollar amount they were looking to spend.

Our customers' ability to pay was always at the forefront. Often, my father would sell a freezer full of meats to one customer who was stocking up for the month and then turn around and just give away something to a family that just didn't have the money.

These were the basics at our market. And as it turns out, my father and grandfather, neither of whom had any more than a few years of high school education, were practicing the basics of customer marketing.

Later, when I was studying marketing at Boston University, I learned that being successful with marketing meant getting a fundamental understanding of who the customer was and what their needs were. It was a little more complicated than working at the family butcher shop, but still all about being in the service of the customer—understanding why they shopped, where they shopped, and what price they were willing to pay.

As I continued through my career, I developed a keen understanding of customer needs in a wide variety of categories—from soda to jeans to software to energy to the lottery; from health care to biotech, wellness, and cannabis. No matter what category, if you have a customer-first orientation—keeping their interests and needs always at the forefront—they will buy what you're selling. And guess what? If your product does what it's supposed to do, they will buy it again and again and again.

"Getting it right" means understanding why customers become repeat buyers. One of the most potent social currencies in society, especially in the world of social media, is to tell others about the products one loves. If it is a new product, the social currency of being the first to try it is compelling. If you are customer-first, your customers will love your product, they will become brand advocates and tell as many of their friends (and non-friends) as they can about it.

Getting it right does not require a massive budget, big agencies, or big brands. It simply requires a willingness to be in the service of your customer—to understand their truths and to be open to pivoting off an idea to make it better.

2. Not Getting It Right

It has become common knowledge and a little cliché, but 90 percent of all new products fail.[2] You'll read later that most of the time, a product fails because there is no market for it, or it does not solve a customer need. While that tends to be the problem, it is a symptom of something more deeply wrong.

Instead of finding out if a market exists, product developers often just assume that it does, probably from their own experience or one-off observations they might see in the store or read online. I can't tell you how many times I have had a conversation with or received a note from a C-suite executive asking why we weren't making one product or another.

That's because everyone mistakenly thinks that they are their target customer. Sometimes that's true, but most often not so much. Product developers and marketers typically don't fit the dominant demographic in most markets in the United States.

The Nagging Problem

The nagging problem is the lack of commitment to do the work necessary to Get It Right.

A customer-first orientation and a solid knowledge base of what customers are seeking and what they want to hear are necessary to be successful.

In 1993, Apple built the Newton Personal Digital Assistant. It was a brilliant product with all of the basic functionality of many of today's phones and tablets. And, it had a cool form factor and a stylus pen. Most importantly, it was designed to solve customer problems.

But Apple made a critical mistake. They said it was a note-taker that could convert your handwriting to text. "We barely got it functioning by '93 when we started shipping it," remarked Steve Capps, Newton's head of user interface.

The Newton, as great a product as it was, was a bust. It did not do what Apple said it could—which was function as a note-taker with handwriting recognition. Newton's character recognition was behind its ultimate failure and was the brunt of many very public jokes, including a week's worth of commentary from Doonesbury.[3] The promise of the product was never fulfilled, and it suffered from user disappointment.

On the other hand, look at what Apple did with the iPod and later with iTunes. Apple did not overreach. The iPod did what it said it could do. And it solved the customer need that the Walkman first had. It made music portable. In the long run, as we all know, the iPod would change the way we all listen to music. Apple knew what customers were looking for (being able to take their music with them anywhere and conveniently buy music) and what they wanted to hear (e.g., a thousand songs in your pocket).

3. Marketing Research

Marketing research is the foundation of any successful marketing plan, and it is essential to continually refer back to the research and insights as you develop your plan. This process of incorporating research in your planning facilitates the creation of great marketing.

Marketing research empowers you to be customer-first. It is in service of the customer and is about translating and communicating the customer's voice to marketers and innovators. It brings the voice of the customer to the boardroom, to the conference room, to the product developers, to the ad agencies, and to the sales teams.

The reason why you do market research is to find nuggets of knowledge that reveal customer intent. There are those who, like the late Apple founder Steve Jobs, say that people don't know what they want until you show it to them. To quote Henry Ford, "If you had asked people what they wanted, they would have said faster horses," because they could not conceive of the automobile—more likely, they probably would have said faster, more comfortable travel that didn't smell like the back of a horse. It is the marketer and innovator's job to figure out what to do with that knowledge.

Whether through trend analysis, traditional market research, or prototype development, great market research guides and shapes your work. It doesn't do your work for you, but it will get you a long way there.

4. JW's Marketing Wheel of Fortune

Excellent product-market fit has been identified by many as the fundamental ingredient for success. The marketing wheel on which I lean when I work with clients takes a dynamic and cumulative approach to how marketing works. It is ordered in such a way as to identify and improve product-market fit.

Build from a place of knowledge and insight. Understand the marketplace, identify your customer and position, and create your products to meet your customers' needs. Build a strategy. Make the purchase experience so right that they'll want to buy your product, and re-enforce the experience with positive messaging. Price it so that they can buy it again. Measure the impact of what you've done, optimize spend, and re-invest back into the business.

JW's Marketing Wheel of Fortune

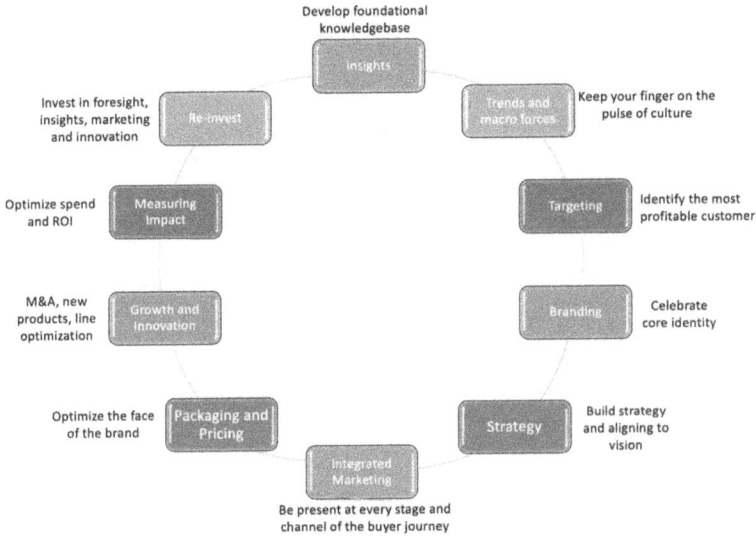

5. Some of What's to Come

In this book, I will lay out my thinking around the art and science of marketing by presenting easy-to-build, easy-to-apply, and easy-to-execute frameworks built from widely established, tried-and-true methods.

Insight

In many chapters, I will show how to apply the insights born from market research. Though I will offer some thoughts, this book is not about how to do market research. It's about how to apply learning from market research to building marketing strategy.

At points along the way, I hope to illustrate the challenges and tensions that face researchers and their clients when making choices.

Macro Forces

Every business needs context. Understanding the market forces and trends helps you leverage your environment to your advantage. Market forces help you establish and create your brand purpose, your mission, and your strategy, and help shape your decision making.

Targeting

Identifying the right and most profitable customer involves more than just identifying who they are and where to find them. It also means getting to know them to understand their pain points and the problems they are looking to solve. It involves understanding their motivations, what kind of content they're attracted to, and whom they trust the most. Targeting is foundational to brand building.

This chapter will explore how to think about simple and complex ways to identify your target customers.

Branding

Brand building is the creative expression of your brand as perceived by the target customer. It's a blend of art and science. It is expressive, and it is common sense. It is about talking to customers in ways that are relevant to them.

This chapter illustrates how to use one version of the brand pyramid to build a brand identity.

Strategy

Smart marketing starts with a solid and grounded strategy. Drawn from data and insights, building strategy involves a thorough review of your strengths, weaknesses, amplifiers, and threats. It is tied back to the mission and vision of the company—every element of the marketing plan is anchored to it.

This chapter will explore how to use the SWAT analysis to build marketing strategy.

Integrated Marketing

Integrated marketing *is* marketing. It is the marketing that reaches out to potential customers to make them aware of your product. It is the marketing that persuades them to purchase, to drive positive user experience, to build loyalty and advocacy. Integrated marketing is defining and aligning marketing tactics to the buyer journey.

Understanding that buyer journey means identifying where your customers spend their time and in what order. It is the top of the funnel down to the bottom of the funnel.

This chapter asks you to think of the funnel as a recursive and continuous journey that starts with awareness and continues through loyalty and advocacy.

Then, this chapter presents ways of thinking about activating your marketing plan.

Packaging and Pricing

Packaging and pricing are how buyers will become exposed to many products for the first time. Whether online or in the store, the visual expression of the package is how they will form their first impressions of the product. They will see your product as expressed by the package and its price. Potential buyers can't avoid "judging a book by its cover." In those early moments, a potential customers will decide based on what it looks like and how much it costs, whether they will consider the product. We all do it.

In this chapter, we will explore some fundamental concepts of how these two aspects of the four P's shape how the customer views the brand.

Measurement

Marketers need measurement. Beyond sales metrics, marketers need to know which tactics are working and which are not. Optimizing the marketing plan is critical to being successful, both from an effectiveness standpoint and a financial resources standpoint.

This chapter focuses on how to look at metrics that help to optimize spend, as well as how to identify metrics that will be useful for understanding marketing effectiveness.

Growth

Growth from M&A and innovation is complex. Time horizons, levels of sophistication, idea development, design thinking, concept testing, brand architecture, and strategic fit are just some of the levers and lenses discussed in this chapter.

6. Marketing Is Fun

Marketing is fun and rewarding. It involves creativity, collaboration, inspiration, discipline, and timing. It reflects culture, and to some extent, it has the ability to shape culture.

We tend to think about marketing as only advertising and innovation, but it is much more than that. Out of it comes great products, great storytelling, and happy customers. And there is nothing more satisfying than making someone else happy.

"If you form a strategy without research, your brand will barely float; and at the speed industries move at today, brands sink fast."
—Ryan Holmes

CHAPTER 2

I Love Market Research

1981

I love market research. I love everything about it. I love learning. I love the numbers. I love the tools. I love the topics, the problems, the storytelling and solutions. I wish everyone loved research as much as I do.

When I went to business school, I focused on marketing. But, like most sophomores in college, I hadn't figured out how my future looked. I had written a business plan to take over the family business, and it was pretty good. The old man and the old man's old man both approved. I think they saw a chance to stop working sooner rather than later.

But then, one day, my business statistics teacher, who was also my house Resident Assistant, suggested that if I liked numbers and marketing, I might really like marketing research. He connected me to a graduate professor at BU—Kevin Clancy (twenty years later, I would later go on to become a Vice President in his company). Clancy connected me with a former student and executive at Booz Allen & Hamilton, where I was offered a market research summer internship.

During that internship, I would write a regression program (using punch cards in Fortran, no less) and edit questionnaires in the research department.

But, the most fun I had was looking at the results of a Xerox customer satisfaction study. The data plus the written comments added such incredible texture to how Xerox repair reps were working with their customers—which included an alleged romantic relationship between the tech and the customer (lots of visits and glowing reviews!).

I went back to school, audited Clancy's graduate market research class, and started doing everything I could to learn about research, including doing street intercepts in the Boston Commons and phone interviewing during dinnertime. I took a job that rotated me through every research job function. I developed an interest in advanced analytics, learned multivariate analysis from books and journals, and became adept at seeing patterns and relationships in data. I couldn't get enough.

Good market researchers *want* to learn. They are curious; they love to dig deeply into the data. They take an extra moment to examine the next relationship, the next tab and correlation. And when they are satisfied, they start building and telling stories about what they have learned.

I don't like to proselytize (much), but I love market research, and more often than not, doing it is worth the time and effort invested in it.

1. So, What Is Market Research?

Market research is any kind of learning that focuses on the marketplace. It can focus on marketing, branding, web development, sales, operations, category management, advertising—any and every kind of study or tool intended to improve your business.

It ranges from the subtlety of observation to the blocking and tackling of data analytics, the rigor of surveying customers, and the genius of advanced analytics and artificial intelligence.

Marketing research has been around for quite a long time, even in the movies. In 1957, Katherine Hepburn and Spencer Tracy starred in the film, *Desk Set*, where Hepburn played Bunny Watson, who is in charge of the Federal Broadcasting reference library responsible for researching facts and answering questions on all manner of topics, great and small. She had a card catalog full of answers. She and her team were market researchers.

The Desk Set: old-school research in action.

Don't be fooled into thinking that market research is only surveys. It's anything you can do to learn about the market to improve business.

Market research has evolved into a field that is more about insights than about data. But even more than that, the real work is to identify business problems, design and execute the data collection and analysis, and build the stories based on the insights drawn from the data. Those insights are the product of the work and the foundation for developing plans, decision making, and marketing strategy.

Market researchers, with time in their roles, have seen most marketing, innovation, and sales problems there are to see. Why? Because they are the hub. While marketing teams do rotations, researchers work on the entire business. They see all of the problems. Even some CMOs never participate in marketing and sales in the same way.

This applies to marketing research consultants as well. These consultants have seen all of the same problems across a wide range of categories.

Market researchers see everything.

2. The Power of Market Research

There is nothing more powerful than understanding your customer, having competitive insights, and knowing how and where to spend your money. You build your strategy on information, you make decisions based on information, and you course-correct based on that information. Every action you perform improves with credible information.

Start-ups, which tend not to have a great deal of information, time, patience, or money, make decisions using much smaller subsets of information. But they have to do it. It is expected and necessary.

A simple example: I was working with a start-up that needed more revenue from its direct-to-customer e-commerce business. They believed that they understood their customers and felt their website was working. We did a simple survey of those who had visited their website, supported by analysis using Google Analytics, and boom—we had the insights necessary to improve the site and to optimize purchasing and check-out. It is straightforward, compelling stuff.

3. Insights: The Cassandra Crossing

My favorite story about insights starts with Cassandra. She was the daughter of King Priam and Queen Hecuba of Troy, and she was one of the most beautiful princesses of Troy.

Cassandra, *by* Evelyn De Morgan *(1898, London)*
Cassandra in front of the burning city of Troy

The story goes that Apollo, the son of Zeus, fell madly in love with Cassandra. Though she did not have the powers of an immortal god, she coveted them. So, she made a deal with Apollo. In exchange for her affection, he gave her the power of foresight.

As happens with these kinds of matches, things didn't work out well between the two of them. Once Cassandra was given the power of foresight, she spurned Apollo's advances. Apollo was not happy about the situation and placed a curse upon her.

Apollo allowed her to keep her gift but deprived her of the ability to persuade—no matter the situation. Being a princess of Troy, this turned out pretty badly for all concerned. Cassandra warned that Paris would destroy Troy, that Helen would be the cause, and that there was an enemy army inside a wooden horse (more or less). Cassandra had foreseen the destruction of Troy but was unable to get anyone to believe her.

Market researchers can feel like Cassandra—having a deep understanding of data and outcomes but finding that the audience is difficult to convince. As the old saying goes, "You can lead a horse to water, but you can't make it drink."

We know, realistically, that market researchers cannot perfectly predict the future. If we could, we'd all be wealthy—investing in the best products before they come out, finding the right companies and the best clients. Speaking from personal experience, that's just not the case.

Insights are the result of seeing or apprehending the inner nature of things.

One of my favorite illustrations about insights comes from a famous sports drink brand. In the 1990s, this major brand felt its target customer was the athlete—not just the everyday athlete, but the professional athlete.

The market research illustrated how the athlete, in turn, talked about how they used the drink, how they carried it, when they drank it, and how it was always with them when they needed it.

The insight was that, for athletes, a sports drink was not just a drink, but a part of their life and their toolkit for success.

The insight is the meaning drawn from the data.

Businesses of every type have come to realize the value of data and the resulting insights. Those insights can improve the chances of marketing and innovation success, mitigating the pitfalls and stumbles and insulating the company, as best as possible, from failure.

According to ESOMAR, a not-for-profit organization that promotes the value of markets, opinion, and social research, as well as data analytics, the size of the global market research industry was $76 billion in 2017.[4]

Insights are valuable, because having objective data is how you launch your brand, your market positioning, and your go-to-market strategy. When you build your brand around objective data, you build your brand around the customer. That means the data has to represent the authentic voice of the customer.

When you echo the voice of the customer, your brand begins to resonate, and you become a customer-centric company.

When you are customer-centric, everything you do is in the service of the customer. Your customer will recognize it and respond favorably to it.

That is the purpose of market research and the purpose of customer-first insights. A customer-centric business puts the needs of the customer front and center—in innovation, marketing, sales, and even hiring practices.

Several online commerce outlets have gone to great lengths to instill a customer-first strategy in their DNA. Consider:

- The Zappos vision is to deliver happiness to customers, employees, and vendors.
- Similarly, Amazon's vision statement is "to be Earth's most customer-centric company."

For CPG marketing, customer-centric marketing is so vital that fully funded brand research agendas (representing as much as 7 percent of the brand budget) are set aside at the beginning of each planning year.

But money is only part of the issue.

4. The Politics of Insight

Researchers may have a holier-than-thou attitude, and feel like they are there to protect the truth — to keep the data from being misused and to keep marketers on the straight and narrow. To some extent, this is true, but mostly it is misguided. Researchers don't own the truth.

The researcher's responsibility is to clearly communicate what they know, and advise, as simply as possible, to help shape decision making collectively with their partners and clients.

On countless occasions, insights professionals are conflicted. They want to help their colleagues achieve their original plans but know those plans need adjustment. The principal goal must always be to help make marketing and innovation be the best that they can be, collectively, and not to care how you got there, only *that* you got there.

The desire to deliver the insights and balance them with the goals of those client partners is challenged by changing priorities, agendas, and egos.

I have worked with innovators who are pressured to bring new products to market and whose chief motivation is to launch profitable new products. Their intentions, for the most part, are always the same. Get to market fast, get the product moving with marketing, and move on to the next one.

Those intentions can sometimes get in the way of making the right decision. I have been in meetings where we look at the same data, and they see "launch" when the data says "don't launch." Understand that it's hard to course-correct late in the game—time and money have been spent, the deadlines are real, and the resources are in line to execute the next step.

I have seen food products for humans and for pets that were not ready for the market but were pushed to launch. Pepsi Blue lasted only two years on the market. There are other instances, like the Apple Newton, Del Monte Fruit Cups, Nike Fuel, and the Sega DreamCast.[5] And, of course, there is the famous Levi's Leisure Suit.

In this last example (an HBR classic),[6] the Leisure Suit was the pet project of a member of the Haas Family—the majority owners of Levi Strauss. Leadership was gathered at a focus group facility, sitting behind the one-way mirror and observing the moderator and the group discuss the leisure suit.

In no uncertain terms, the participants in the group said they did not like the idea. But, despite clearly hearing directly from customers' mouths that they weren't interested in the product, they pushed the launch forward. It did not do well.

The pressure to launch a new marketing campaign will come under the same kind of scrutiny. And, mind you, you don't hear about the success stories. But, at Big Heart Pet Brands, the marketing campaigns for almost all of our brands were optimized using cutting-edge insight tools to improve their success and return on investment. That doesn't mean there wasn't conflict.

The tension between the pressure to execute and to respond to learning is always challenging.

5. Tension Is Good. Facts Are Better.

In 2007, Kevin Clancy and Peter Krieg authored *Your Gut Is Still Not Smarter Than Your Head: How Disciplined, Fact-Based Marketing*

Can Drive Extraordinary Growth and Profits. The essence of the book is pretty evident from the title—marketers need to make decisions based on research, information, and guidance rather than on what their gut is telling them.

That is the essence of the tension between the marketer and the market researcher—and it's the source for the politics of insight. Here are two examples:

- Corporate innovation teams who are under pressure to create value and grow the business sometimes cut corners so they can get to market quickly.

  As part of this, they use the insights to validate why they believe the product will be successful, as opposed to how to make it successful.

  This causes a fair amount of tension.

- Advertising agencies have historically appreciated research as a way to provide fodder for creatives to develop great thematic advertising. However, most ad agencies do not believe that research will be an accurate reflection of how the tested ads will perform in the market.

Marketers are in their job to be creative and to push the boundaries of creation—to find new ways to communicate, innovate, and go to market that do not always seem obvious.

The old stereotype of market researchers being linear, pragmatic, and unbending gets in the way of a true partnership.

The researcher needs to bring the creative marketer into the process so that they can actively participate and co-create—balancing the truth and responsibility with the goals of the brand.

6. Guidance for the Researchers

Trust, Independence & Courage

The tension that comes from facing off with internal and external clients is born from the researcher's need to maintain trust and independence.

Researchers walk a fine line. Clients and organizational leaders need to know that they can trust the recommendations and commitment of the insights team—that they will be truthful and portray findings without personal bias.

Trust is an essential characteristic for an insights professional. To support a team or organization, stay true to the learning and don't let personal biases about a program or product affect the conclusion. Researchers need to have opinions, but they have to share their thoughts in the context of learning without an agenda.

Clients must see the researcher as independent from others who have agendas. Research is not done to substantiate personal opinions; it is done to test them.

Linked to these two, the researcher must have the courage to challenge convention, even senior management. "Better to be known a fool by speaking than thought a fool by not speaking." Clients have to know that they can expect the researcher to speak up when the data and insights they have generated say something different than what clients wanted to hear.

Early in my time at Pepsi, I was in awe of the Pepsi leadership team, perhaps even suffering from a bit of imposter syndrome. I know there were times when I should have spoken up at the leadership table, and I didn't. Sitting back quietly hurt my credibility. Leadership has to trust that you know that speaking up is in the best interest of the team.

Sheryl Sandberg's book *Leaning In* is relevant to everyone, but market researchers, who tend to be a little on the quiet side, will find it particularly helpful.

Marketers and researchers often face off on opposite sides of a point. Sometimes the researcher, when faced with unwavering opposition, must find a compromise. Business and market realities, such as they are, require agility, and not all problems can be solved with the insights from research. So, marketing researchers need to be team players. The client team needs to know that you are there to help them work through the issues with them—as part of the team. It's too easy to be critical and point out what's wrong, and it's not always easy to find ways to fix it.

The Wharton School of Business offers a course on Strategic Persuasion. The principal focus is on listening. Listen. Put yourself in your partner's shoes. Understand their challenges and point of view.

Researchers need to be agile enough to find solutions, compromise, and support the eventual vetted strategies and direction—even if there are differing opinions. In other words, walk out of the room together focused on a shared goal with a common understanding of the data.

Good researchers need to be courageous, independent, and trustworthy partners who have a track record of telling the truth so that clients want to listen to and believe what they say.

Consider the work at Del Monte and Big Heart Pet Brands. The research team was trained on how to handle tension, to work collaboratively, to remain agnostic and focused on the shared goals of the organization. This collaboration generated an increased appreciation for the team and for the value of knowledge.

Eventually, Del Monte was acknowledged as a finalist for an international award for the Most Knowledgeable Enterprise, because everyone embraced insights, despite the tension and conflicts that might have arisen.

7. Storytelling

Delivering unbiased insights and truth is challenging because many times, the results are not what people want to hear. Nobody likes being told they are wrong. Great researchers have to understand that data tells a great story, and that the best way to communicate the results is through storytelling.

Being a great listener, collaborator, communicator, and storyteller should break the tension between researcher and marketer and generate great marketing.

8. A Broken Record

Many companies try to use old research to solve current problems, and some try to validate their old practices with new research. But markets change with new competitors, new products. And new trends are emerging all the time. Companies need to use research to identify and direct future practices, not confirm old ones.

Your research doesn't have to be perfect. The amount of time and money it takes to be perfect would make any research undertaking counter-productive and too expensive.

Unbiased and well-communicated insight work informs strategy, positioning, innovation, and go-to-market decision making. Using resources wisely and collecting the most pertinent data enables you to be proactive and get ahead of the competition.

"Great brands don't just ride shifts in culture; they contribute to them."
—Reid Hoffman

CHAPTER 3

The Future Defines the Present

2007

The wall behind me is a gorgeous blue. It is about fifteen feet high, it stretches about thirty feet to each side of me, and nestled inside the center is a vibrant gigantic display. On both sides, the wall is curved like the blade of a hockey stick, so that it gently hugs me.

It's lit from the bottom up, so that images of Bono, a hybrid car, a young family, and more are gentle teases of what we hope to accomplish.

I look out at the audience—well, not the audience yet. All I can see is black. We are in a black box theater. The stage is sunken, and the risers present a Greek theater style of seating. All eyes will be on me. Well, maybe not me; rather, they will be on the wall and the enormous video screen behind me. It's time for Crashing the Culture.

It is not the first time I have delivered a presentation like this. I've been with Pepsi for a good long time. I understand the people, but this is a departure. This is entertainment. Content mixed with entertainment. This is corporate edutainment—more than just a presentation, it is communicating content so that people will remember and want to use the learning.

The audience begins to arrive. We're in New York, at Pepsi Headquarters. Tropicana will be polite. Frito Lay, collaborative. Gatorade, indifferent. But Pepsi, they are quintessential New York; not so much "show me" as "prove it." And in a way, that is the point of all of this. Trends are simply entertainment if not harnessed properly. They will fall flat, and the audience will be disappointed, but more importantly, dismissive of the learning. The work will be for naught.

Crashing the Culture was designed to bring the latest trends relevant to the Food & Beverage category to help shape innovation and marketing. These kinds of trends programs have a synergistic effect across an organization. Bringing groups together to discuss the opportunities and challenges is morale-boosting, team building, and educational.

That first year, in true Pepsi fashion, the program was equal parts theater and insight. Actors and singers were brought in from off-Broadway to demonstrate the learning in a highly visceral way. Scripts and vignettes described what we needed to communicate. The program was a success on many accounts. It reflected a new way to deliver learning, and more importantly, our audience used the data.

The program was so successful that I re-created the program for Del Monte and Big Heart Pet Brands. We "hacked" the name, and called it Hacking the Culture.

1. Trends Are the Trend

Everyone loves trends. They're fun and entertaining, and they represent societal cultural markers. Companies like The Faith Popcorn Brain Reserve, Purple Telescope, Trendhunter.com, Trendwatching.com, The Institute for the Future, and many, many others have been developing and explaining the nature and importance of trends for decades.

Trends are important markers of how culture has changed, and markers of how categories have changed in more specific ways. Trends are the canvas on which marketing and innovation are painted.

The way to think about trends is really to identify the prevailing cultural movement in the collective mindset of the population. This can be either in total, in a particular category, or even in a micro-segment.

Each trend and its resulting interpretation has its basis in fact. There is power in understanding societal trends.

- There are broad trends, like Cocooning, that represent how families are closing up ranks to protect themselves from the unpredictable realities of the outside world. One wonders what Covid-19's shelter-in-place orders will evolve into next.

- #MeToo and #TimesUp emerged alongside the evolution of women's role in business and the evolving distrust of icons and institutions. The lack of trust in government has expanded into a lack of confidence in big tech and big business. Banks and oil companies are no longer the only big villains.

As examples of how trends become fertile places for innovation and communication, let's consider these meaningful trends that are still in play today.

- **Simplification of Complexity**: The population is looking for simplicity, not complexity. Faith Popcorn once told me that people would soon start paying more to get less. Muji defined simplicity as one of its core values. Some customers consider smaller sizes as a sign of quality and scarcity. Some will pay more for less because they simply don't want or need more.

- **Authenticity/Lack of Trust**: Pervasive in every aspect of life, people are looking for authenticity in their leaders, in their CEOs, and especially in their brands. This means "walking the talk." Dove's Real Beauty campaign chose to take an authentic road to beauty, regardless of age.

- **The Democratization of Everything**: Everybody feels entitled to have access to everything. That means a sense of entitlement for luxury items—which spawned a whole new world of accessible luxury. Think Vera Wang at Kohl's department store. Or, the Mazda 3 sports car with all the bells and whistles of the more expensive but similarly featured Audi A3.

- **Holistic Living**: This exploded into and created a new way of thinking about how we live our lives. Wellness is not just about physical health, but mental and spiritual health as well. It has created more focus on the origin of food and how it is grown. Take, for example, the Hawaiian Ola beverage company. Hawaiian Ola is a certified B-Corporation, which means it is held to higher standards of social and environmental performance, transparency, and accountability. Hawaiian Ola manufactures coffee, tea, and energy shot drinks that support Hawaii's environment and economy by empowering local farmers producing organic, responsibly grown crops.

There are categorical trends, too, that show how customers' purchasing and attitudes are changing.

- The vast Health and Wellness trend started in foods with low-calorie ingredients, then moved to low-calorie, no harmful ingredients, and then to being "plussed up" with origin stories and sustainability credentials. It has fast become a much larger macro trend splitting off into multiple mini-trends.

Trends are also markers of how quickly times can change.

- One only needs to look at the new millennium. We had a liberal political environment; the economy was turning; racism and women's movements were coming to the forefront. Just a few years later, the political climate becomes conservative; there is significant misinformation and a broad lack of trust. The women's movement, however, has been fueled by and accelerated through this change.

We see trends evolve, converge, and diverge all the time. But, for brand marketers and innovators, a trend worth chasing is grounded in sound thinking and is one that has emerged over time. It has substance. It is rooted in fact, and it is not conjectured and not "spun."

2. Trends Evolve, but Forces Are Ever Present

The strength of an idea—and its ultimate success in the market—is heavily influenced by the market and cultural forces that surround it. As marketers and innovators, nothing we do happens in isolation.

Trends are the inspiration behind innovation and messaging. Smart marketers take advantage of the trends of the day, and architect new companies, missions, marketing messages, and products.

Market forces can best be understood as economic, technological, political, and environmental. Both trends and market forces are influential and can be leveraged to a company's advantage—to co-create alongside.

While trends are cultural, and tend to be belief-driven and more shapeable, they also tend to be drawn from the creative seed within a larger market force.

Age Magnified

Age as a market force affects virtually every aspect of marketing and innovation. It can serve as a means for targeting, assessing needs, creating new products and creating new ways to communicate. Age is the very best example of a predictable long-term market.

Basic math allows us easily to know, at any given time, how many people there will be in each age bracket at any time in the future.

Lifestage

Lifestage marketing suggests that everyone is on a bigger journey— that each of us is on a path that leads us through different milestones in our lives.

- Young adults start dating.
- Newlyweds start households and buy homes.
- Young couples share pets instead of children.
- Other young couples do have children.
- Those children begin to grow up.
- Kids go to college.
- Those young parents are now empty nesters (with time, energy, and money to burn).
- Finally, those older adults become grandparents and have health problems and need more medical care.
- And then, like all things, their lives come to an end, leaving their children to handle the arrangements.

And the cycle repeats.

From a macro-force perspective, the marketer can focus on lifestage to build programs.

- Young parents will need diapers.
- Empty nesters will be looking for new experiences.
- Older adults with aging parents are struggling with end-of-life issues.

If you are a beverage company, you know that

- Children drink milk.
- Tweens drink soda.
- Teens experiment with new beverages.
- College-age kids experiment with alcohol.
- Young adults refine their beverage tastes for alcohol and nonalcoholic beverages.
- Young marrieds drink more healthily.
- And so on.

For every life stage, you pretty much know what's coming. More than likely, you can predict spending and consumption patterns for most customer categories. So, lifestage is an excellent canvas on which to paint. It is a force that will simply never go away.

Age expressed by cohorts and life stage is a powerful platform for development, and you can begin to appreciate why understanding those patterns as predictable macro forces can help tailor your strategy, product, and communications.

Political Magnifiers

The Cyclical Nature of Society

Generations are a worthy market force to track because they too, are predictable and cyclical. Authors William Strauss and Neil Howe describe a theory of recurring generation cycles in American history in *Generations*, which was published in 1991.[7]

Every generation has its social, political, and economic challenges. Going back to as early as 1584, Strauss and Howe illustrated how generations tend to be formed in cyclical patterns. These patterns were described as "turnings" and were defined by significant world events, including the Great Depression, World War II, the Vietnam War, September 11, and now COVID-19, to name the ones with which Americans are most familiar.

The First Turning is defined as a "High," which is a period after a crisis that tests the will of the public and challenges its collective identity. In response to the crisis, society forms strong bonds to reaffirm the collective will of the people. This is a period of growth.

The Second Turning, the "Awakening," begins when personal autonomy, stifled mainly in the name of collectivism, begins to emerge again.

The Third Turning, the "Unraveling," is where institutions are weak and distrusted, and individualism is healthy and flourishing.

In the Fourth Turning, eventually, distrust among institutions grow to a point where they can no longer be tolerated.

Their other books, *Millennials Rising* and *The Fourth Turning*, builds upon this theory. *The Fourth Turning* was especially prescient, predicting an event (9/11) that would rally a generation and cause boomers to grapple with the dilemma of letting their children go to war.

The cyclical nature of society is predictable. At the time of this writing, we are in the current cycle of a Fourth Turning. Before COVID-19, trust in government and among institutions had eroded. And now, the mass worldwide protests behind Black Lives Matter represent a significant change in the way the new generation is shaping culture. All this will lead to another First Turning—a response to crisis where the collective will of the people is expressed.

Each time a new cycle takes hold, the pulse of the population changes. It is crucial for the health of business to stay on top of these in order to relate and communicate with your customers.

Immigration Waves

Immigration has an ongoing influence on society and is another macro force to track.

Insular communities that don't speak any English need to be marketed to in a completely different way. They require special packaging and advertising that is in a language that they can understand. And, the messages and products must be supportive of their economic mindset. In the absence of that, these buyers tend to just purchase based on familiarity.

The third-generation ethnic cohorts are more similar to the mainstream population when they make purchasing decisions. The second-generation ethnic cohorts are working on assimilating and are making decisions that help them with learning the culture.

In particular, immigration, since the founding of the United States, has occurred along multiple ethnic waves. As an illustration:

- Between 1525 and 1866, in the entire history of the slave trade to the New World, according to the Trans-Atlantic Slave Trade Database, 12.5 million Africans were taken to the New World by ship. Of these, close to 400,000 were taken directly to North America.
- The immigrants to arrive from England and Northern Europe came in the seventeenth century up until the founding of the United States.
- Irish and Germans started coming in big numbers in the 1840s.
- In the late 1800s and early 1900s, immigration again skyrocketed, mostly from Southern and Eastern Europe.
- Immigration slowed for decades after the passage of the Immigration Act of 1924.
- In 1965, Johnson passed the Immigration Act of 1965, which opened the door for large-scale immigration from Latin America and Asia.

As a market force, each time a new immigration cycle takes hold, the tapestry of America changes. Unique needs arise, and the need to communicate more inclusively is required.

Economic and Societal Magnifiers

The forces of economic, social, and political events that occurred during these generations magnify the impact of macro forces when they come together.

The economy has two pretty clear effects on society. The momentum of the economy is what drives spending and customer confidence. When the economy is moving, most everyone is benefiting. All industries are firing on all cylinders, and it is a ripe opportunity within which to sell and innovate.

The second effect of the economy is no subtler or more dramatic. For at least two decades, we have seen a widening gap between the "haves" and the "have-nots." What is worse is that this gap has become exacerbated in recent years.

The importance of value alternatives and value pricing is shaping how portfolios are being developed. It is also shaping how products are being messaged.

I remember working with the president of a large CPG on a short pricing study to find ways to bundle, package, or price products in such a way as to make them more affordable for more people.

Different packaging bundles were shaped out of the "have" and "have-not" needs in the economy. For the "haves": premium pricing with higher margins. For the "have-nots": value pricing at lower margins. The higher-margin products provide the ability to price more accessibly at the bottom end of the portfolio.

Technology

Technology is one of the single most disruptive macro forces, and together with other forces and trends, it has the power to create monumental change. Consider:

- The speed of technological innovation and how it's affected data storage: from CDs to DVDs, to thumb and flash drives, and now to the cloud.

- The speed of data and the internet and how it changed the way we work. We started in the office, then with flex time, then telework from home, at the café, and finally to coworking spaces like WeWork.

- Packaging evolution and how milk that was once delivered in glass bottles to your doorstep is now being sold in recycled cardboard boxes.

- Facebook, Google, and Twitter—and how we access information. They've created a zeitgeist of uninterrupted access to information.

Gaming

What was once a category just for fun, gaming has exploded into a significant macro force. Gaming is a $116 billion industry and recently eclipsed television as the most popular form of home entertainment. Gaming's presence now ranges from global sports leagues to corporate training.

Like many generations, Gen-Xer's, the millennial generation and Gen-Z grew up with video games, and remain some of the heaviest users of them.[8] In their formative years, Nintendo, Gameboy, Sony PlayStation, and Sega were experiencing enormous acceptance and growth. Personally, I remember playing Sega's *Sonic the Hedgehog* the way younger generations played *Super Mario*.

As these generations matured, their heart for gaming never left them. They still play at home. As nostalgia starts to play a bigger role in these consumers' lives, the partnerships brands make with gaming can net significant exposure.

Millennials and Gen-Xers have also taken their interest in gaming to work. Gaming has proven to be a popular and effective form of employer-based training.

A study by the University of Colorado Denver Business School found that using video games in training led to substantial improvements in performance, particularly when the video games actively engaged participants.[9] The researchers analyzed 65 studies and data from 6,476 trainees, focusing on studies that examined post-training outcomes for simulation games. The findings indicated that self-efficacy and knowledge were meaningfully higher for learners trained with simulation games.

Now, newer platforms have emerged. Virtual and augmented reality have become products by themselves. VR and AR tools, like Oculus,[10] are being adopted to improve the way people shop for products. The convergence of emerging technology and gaming will spawn new generations of products and brand applications.

Social (In)Justice

I debated whether or not to include a commentary on social injustice as a macro force in a marketing book. Social injustice is definitely a macro force that is shaping the landscape within which we market and innovate. I don't want to seem disingenuous or somehow to suggest we take advantage of causes just to look good in the customer's eyes. In fact, I'm suggesting just the opposite. Business can help drive change, and with the right kind of positive messaging and innovation, marketing can shape culture and help improve society.

Nike has supported major cultural movements for decades, including LGBTIQA+ rights through Megan Rapinoe, civil rights through Colin Kaepernick, and gender equality through Serena Williams and Title IX. Their deep pockets and deeply resonant advertising have become part of culture.

When companies use their voices to enter these discussions, regardless of what they're selling, customers take notice, and they can help shape society on a grander scale.

Convergence

It's not unusual to have multiple market forces collide. The convergence of age, technology, health & wellness, and financial services will continue to be a potent combination for new product growth.

- As the baby boom generation enters retirement, the solutions that will address its myriad needs will grow in size and complexity. Technology will need to find solutions for in-home care, dementia, and mobility. Retirement portfolios are going to need to be creative to protect and insulate from risk as this generation lives longer than the previous generation.

- Look at the other end of the age spectrum. DNA testing and digestive health are burgeoning areas to meet the needs of growing children. Companies like Brainiac Kids are focusing on providing yogurt-based products that include nutrients for brain health. Evolve Biosystems has developed a probiotic infant formula to improve infant gut health.

- For years, the fast food chains have been trying to find ways to improve their image by serving salads and offering healthier or less indulgent options. Now, Burger King is accelerating through the plant-based trend, by offering meatless Impossible Burgers. Starbucks is doing the same with Beyond Meat.

There is no telling what else will come from the convergence of different trends and forces.

Speed Bumps and Inflection Points

When I was a kid, growing up in Philadelphia, in the fall and winter, we used to play street hockey almost every day after school. Usually, the 10 of us would set up the nets between two-speed bumps in the road. For street hockey, this was very important. When the ball would go beyond the goal, as it often did, the speed bump would slow it down, giving us time to catch it before the ball went into the sewer drain and stalling the game until we could get a new ball.

Similarly, when I was older, we coined the term frisbee traps. So, when we played frisbee in the street, and the frisbee would get by us, the bumps in the road, or the tree, or the sign, or the car side mirror, or the uneven pavement would change the direction of, or even stop, the frisbee.

Inflection points are like speed bumps, or frisbee traps that change the path of a brand or a category—for better or for worse. A new inflection point is in the making for many categories due to COVID-

19. The virus is going to change how we work, where we work, where we eat, what we eat, how we get to get around, and so much more.

- For instance, the global pandemic is spawning new areas of growth in unlikely places. New apps and services are being developed to help the global community remain connected. There is even a senior community service, Radio Recliner, that enables aging nursing home residents to stay connected by allowing them to DJ from their rooms.
- I feel a product recall can permanently damage a brand. The Milo's Kitchen brand of pet treats was launched with great fanfare, strong advertising and recognition as an innovative product. Unfortunately, a recall stalled the growth of the brand and it never really returned to its former glory and trajectory.

Inflection Points: Uber vs. Lyft[11]

Uber and Lyft are perfect expressions of this. UberCab was launched in June of 2010 in San Francisco and was perceived as one of the most innovative start-ups to surface. An early profile in *TechCrunch*, a popular online publication for start-ups, said, "The charges are 1.5x taxi rates, and it's worth it."[12] Uber was solving a major pain point for people just trying to get around town easily and on-demand – without the exchange of currency or the concern over tipping (among other things).

The brand personality was energetic, youthful, and a little brash. In profiling Uber's New York City Headquarters in October of 2016, *Business Insider* commented on the office's energetic culture where employees rode around on skateboards and scooters, the office gathered to eat breakfast together, employees could use the gym on company time, and free beer was served during happy hour.

The brand also had a youthful personality, in part because of the early customers it was attracting. A 2016 article in *The Independent* cited a survey from the Pew Research Center that noted the company was "used almost exclusively by young, university-educated, and wealthy customers."[13]

The company also used aggressive tactics when raising capital in trying to kneecap its competitor, Lyft. In 2014, Kalanick was quoted as saying, "We knew that Lyft was going to raise a ton of money. And we are going [to their investors], 'Just so you know, we're going to be fund-raising after this, so before you decide whether you want to invest in them, just make sure you know that we are going to be fund-raising immediately after."[14]

Then the company matured. Sexual harassment charges emerged, and drivers were involved in a number of actual and alleged crimes.[15] #DeleteUber happened. The corporate culture degraded and employees referred to the headquarters in SF as the "Death Star." Eventually, Kalanick was replaced.

While Uber continues to innovate, the tarnished brand will need some more "polishing."

Contrast that with Lyft. It pretty much does the same thing as Uber. But it started out in a warmer and friendlier place. Its founders are explicitly idealistic about Lyft's mission to eliminate the environmental and financial costs of personal car ownership.

While Uber initially focused on fancy black cars, Lyft let people drive their modest older-model sedans and initially stuck mustaches on the front of the car to reassure passengers that Lyft was goofily benevolent. It invited passengers to ride upfront with the driver, like a friend rather than a customer.

The pink mustache evolved into a pink Lyft logo, and its message was focused on both getting you to your destination and how you got there.

The two brands diverged. Lyft continues to have a much more favorable image. And the image is reflective of its contractor/employee drivers. For the last several years, Harry Campbell and researchers at Stanford University have surveyed 60,000+ drivers to measure things like earnings and what is important to the driver. Throughout this time, Uber drivers have scored lower than Lyft drivers in terms of driver satisfaction.

Inflection points should work in a brand's favor. As we have seen, they don't always. Brands should accelerate through inflection points and ride them to new product development.

3. Futures Work

All of these forces and trends mean something at a given point of time. By looking backward, they give you context for where you might be going.

Futures work is vital work to imagine how brands and categories change. The value of this work is to imagine futures without constraints based on what you know of the past and the present.

At PepsiCo, we did sweeteners futures work to determine what sweeteners would be the healthiest for consumers and have the right flavor profiles for different beverages. From that study, new products were tested and even supply chains were adjusted to make sure we had enough of the right ingredients.

At Big Heart Pet Brands, we imagined the future of feeding dogs. We literally envisioned a time when dogs and their pet parents would be able to communicate. There is quite a bit of science around this already.

4. Back to Crashing the Culture

Aside from my microphone literally dropping to the floor and having to do the rest of the talk without amplification, the event in the black box theater was received exceptionally well. It was more than I could have hoped for, and the audience was collaborative and appreciative. It gave me new insight into the value of not just the trends programs themselves, but how they can change culture.

Crashing the Culture turned into a multi-year trends program in which PepsiCo invested heavily because we believed that trends would help shape the way we went to market. In that first year, we highlighted trends and macro forces that connected the entire organization around these themes. These resulted in new innovation tracks, new marketing communications strategies, and new areas of study.

Hacking the Culture at Del Monte and Big Heart Pet Brands was similar in nature but on a smaller scale. To some extent, perhaps, it was more successful because there was a greater thirst for external stimulus to push marketing and innovation.

5. The Future Defines the Present

Understanding trends helps us paint a picture of what the future might look like, and puts the present in context. Think about it this way—if you have a vision of the future, doesn't it change about how you think about what you should be doing today?

"If you aim at nothing you will hit it every time."

—Zig Ziglar

CHAPTER 4

Birds of a Feather

1997

San Francisco. Classic, Victorian painted lady home. Gorgeous. But I'm in the basement. The basement is dark, with just a thin stream of light coming in from the transom window. I've been deployed to work on a segmentation and targeting consulting gig, partnering with another consultant, for a large apparel company. We've been working on this for weeks.

It's a rich data set. Deep attitude and usage data. Large sample sizes. We can drill deep on any sub-sample.

There's paper (yes, paper) spread out all over the floor. The more we looked, the harder it was to find a solution. There just isn't anything that seems useful for key target identification for the portfolio. Nothing is predictive of how customers shop the portfolio.

K-means, hierarchical, factor, CHAID analyses, and even multi-way cross tabs. Nothing. Nada. Zippo. Zilch. No luck.

Richard McCullough, a lifelong market researcher and close friend, who authored a series of comedic laws of statistics, was in the basement with us. One of McCullough's laws of statistics: "If you torture a data set long enough, it will confess." So, we keep plugging away.

Then, an obvious solution reveals itself. It's simple. It's age. The age of the customer was most predictive how customers shop the portfolio!

Years later, Peter Krieg, an associate of mine from Copernicus, used to say, "Don't overlook the obvious."

1. Who Is This Product For?

It seems pretty obvious—identifying your target customer is crucial to the success of any business. Right? Clients, past and present, seem to overlook the obvious—spending the time to find the people who are most interested in what you have to sell is *the* most important thing you do besides actually making your product.

Your product is always in service of your customers' needs. You can have a great product, and have done all the right things to create it, but if it doesn't meet the needs of your customer, it's not really a great product. Interesting? Yup. Creative? Probably. But not great.

Finding your customer involves understanding what they value, what message will resonate with them, and how it ladders back to your mission of *why you are in business*. These are the people who need your product, who will try it, like it, buy it again, and tell others about it.

You will be in meetings with new product developers, and you will ask them, "Who are we targeting for this product?" And you'll hear answers like boomers, or millennials, or people under twenty-five who work, or women over the age of thirty. Perhaps the answer might be, "People who are looking for a healthier lifestyle" or, "Those who want faster computing, or a smaller phone, or a bigger phone." These are big buckets of people. For instance, there are seventy million boomers and seventy-five million millennials[16]. As the amount of customer data collected increases, the possibilities seem endless.

2. The Cube

In the early days of developing targets and the segmentation that created them, researchers were using only one or two lenses of interest to find their customers. Often, they would be simple ones, like age, awareness, or purchase intent—maybe an attitude such as willingness to try a new product. They are all reliable approaches, but over time, they need to be refined and then improved upon.

We've come to realize that demographics, behaviors, and attitudes need to be combined for effective targeting. The important part is to understand what directly impacts people's interest in your product, their purchase intent, the topic of focus, the amount of money they'll spend, and the profit they'll generate.

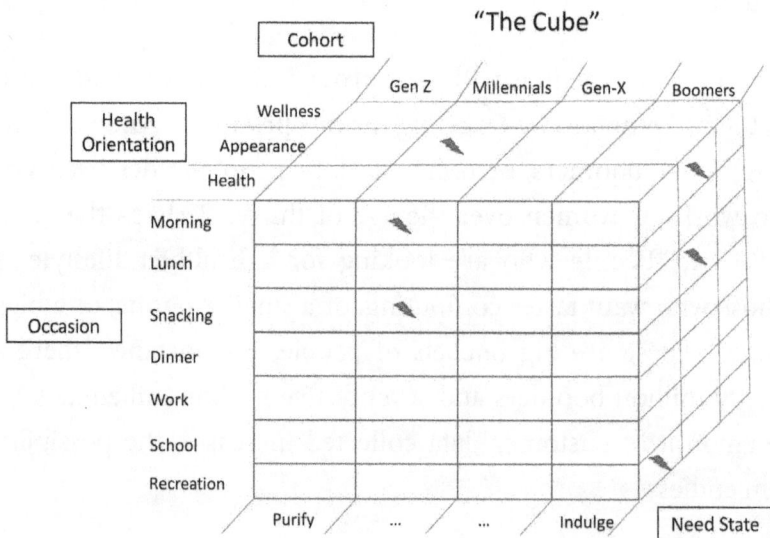

"The Cube"

The cube illustrates how looking at different combinations of variables can reveal pockets of customers who could be most interested in a product or service. It represents how good targeting and segmentation can "light up" (represented by a lightning bolt in the cube) an opportunity represented by one of those cells. But looking at a complex cube, like that one, is pretty ridiculous.

I remember discussing the cube with a few of my colleagues and us all just laughing at how silly it was to even contemplate sharing it with the brand team. While it represented some excellent thinking on each axis, the combinations lacked any simple interpretation or actionability.

The dimensions along the axes of the cube suggest the myriad of potential targeting options that are available when building targets. This is where the cube has real value—illustrating the dimensions on which profitable targets can be built.

3. Targeting Segmentation

In one way or another, businesses always need to identify targets to whom they are selling their product. While, it can be done in a myriad of ways, the one thing they all have in common is that they are all focused on finding an identifiable and findable group of people who find the product or service attractive.

Importantly, these groups' composition makes intuitive sense so that anyone who needs to understand the customer can. They can understand who they are and what makes them tick.

Arriving at your target means that you will be able to find them with your data sources to sell and message to them. It is not always easy if you have a highly complex approach. In the end, the beauty of any method is not only in the target identity, but also that you can effectively reach them. If you can't find/reach them, then what's the point?

Mathematically, there are lots of ways to do it. In the story at the beginning of this chapter, we tried the simple and the sophisticated. What follows is an illustration of the potential dimensions that can fuel the creation of an actionable customer target identification.

4. Drivers

Going back to the cube, there is enormous value in knowing what customer characteristics are the most impactful in driving purchase, profitability, and advocacy.

A great start is simply looking at those variables that are correlated with the key actions that you are trying to drive, like purchase and advocacy. Using those correlated characteristics in your segmentation is a good place to begin.

There is no need to go overboard and create over a thousand individual data variations to identify key drivers. Unless you have a deep analytics bench and time to investigate the data at that depth, staying focused will be more helpful.

Here are some go-to starters that are almost always correlated with some level of action/predictability in customer marketing.

- Descriptive: Journey-Based Dimensions

- Age
- Lifestage
- Generational Cohorts
- Demographic Sub-segments
  - Income
  - Gender Identity
  - Race & Ethnicity
  - Geo-Demographic
- Behavioral/Psychosocial
  - Usage-Based
  - Exhaust Data
  - Occasions
  - Attitudes (Psychographics)
  - Needs

Age, lifestage, ethnicity, and their implied socioeconomic statuses are among the easiest ways to segment a population, because the data is easily obtainable and straightforward—and it is typically associated with an action of intent.

Life's Journey: Age and Lifestage

The knowledge of "when" and "how" families are formed, when children leave the household, and when parents become empty nesters is genuinely actionable. A person's stage in life is comprised of several demographics at once, including age, marital status, and the number of children living in the household.

Think about all the buying decisions that new parents or empty nesters make and how very different those decisions end up. Targeting an age group has worked well for food and beverage companies because the consumption of snacks and drinks tends to be more popular during different stages of life.

Think about the choice of beverage as people age. Young children drink more milk than teenagers do. As they grow older, younger children aspire to drink what the older kids are drinking.

When young adults enter college, many of them discover alcohol. After college, life begins to settle down. Healthier consumption starts to take place. As these young adults mature, they become more focused on quality and style, and opt for wine and spirits. In October 2014, Nielsen Insights reported that when it comes to buying and drinking spirits, customers have a preference for a "delicious and smooth taste" and "stylish" products.[17]

When people become parents, many switch to coffee, or even a diet beverage if they feel it will help them lose a few pounds or stay awake. As people grow older, they tend to drink more coffee. Nearly three-quarters of those age sixty and over report that they drink coffee daily.

That is just one example. Lifestage is an excellent predictor of behavior in many categories. However, it is not the only one to consider.

Generational Cohorts

Generational cohorts are the ultimate bridging variable. Instead of looking at birthday as a life-stage variable, think about it as a way of understanding how people think.

For at least two decades, marketers could not talk about anything else but the baby boomers. That's because there were seventy-six million of them born between 1946 and 1964, representing 40 percent of the US population! Compare this to Generation X (1965-1980), which saw fifty-five million born.[18]

That's still a lot of people, but boomers were the darling target of marketers, in the same way millennials are now, and Gen-Z will be very soon.

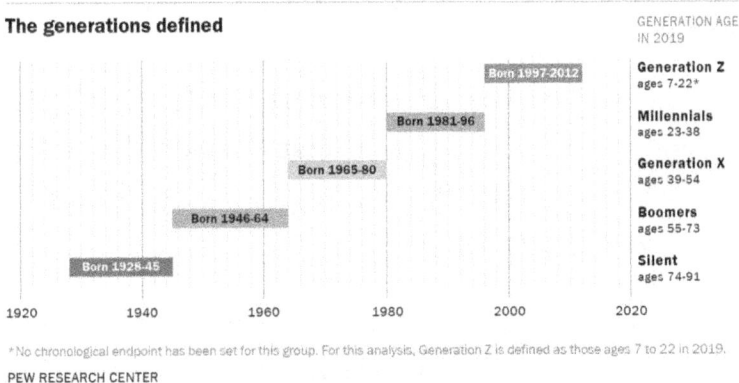

The generations defined

GENERATION AGE IN 2019

Born 1997-2012 — **Generation Z** ages 7-22*

Born 1981-96 — **Millennials** ages 23-38

Born 1965-80 — **Generation X** ages 39-54

Born 1946-64 — **Boomers** ages 55-73

Born 1928-45 — **Silent** ages 74-91

1920   1940   1960   1980   2000   2020

*No chronological endpoint has been set for this group. For this analysis, Generation Z is defined as those ages 7 to 22 in 2019.

PEW RESEARCH CENTER   19

Taking a look at these cohorts will illustrate why they are such great starting points for targeting. It is just too easy! Cohorts represent different ages, ethnicities, lifestages, and attitudes all wrapped up in one. Here's a little texture.

- Boomers – The Greying Tsunami. This is the most famous generation in US history. They are responsible for the civil rights movement and protesting the war in Vietnam, and were the '60s summer-of-love idealists. But they tend to be the most narcissistic and self-centered. Boomers believed and continue to believe that they can create the world around their own needs and attitudes. And they will continue to think that businesses should cater to them.

- Gen-Xers are the latchkey generation characterized by a lot of afterschool video game time until their parents came home from work.

  Called the Lost Generation because of its smaller size, it was overlooked by many marketers. But now, Gen-X has substantial disposable incomes, and according to the Department of Labor, they outspend all other generations when it comes to housing, clothing, eating out, and entertainment.[20] Represented by tech leaders like Jeff Bezos, Sergey Brin, Larry Page, and Susan Wojcicki, they ended up changing the world by founding or leading companies like Amazon, Google, and YouTube.

  Perhaps a little disappointed by brands that had overlooked them when they were in their youth, this generation has set a high bar for brand engagement.

- Millennials are now the second-largest generation in the USA (after baby boomers). They have a global orientation—

and are really the first generation to grow up in a Google world.

- o They are independent (though some of their parents might disagree!), in their peak earning years, and moving from being young adults to forming households with their partners. And, like their boomer parents before them, they are now on the front lines driving social change.

- Gen-Z is massive and is influential. In the USA alone, there are sixty-five million of them. By 2020, Generation Z will account for 40 percent of all customers in the USA..
  - o Gen-Z is into authenticity and relatability, prefers to see real people in ads, and is more interested in seeing people who aren't 100-percent perfect. They are the "Always On" generation. And, of course, heavily influenced by social media. Tik Tok is a brand practically created for them.

So, many marketers are satisfied with generational cohorts for targeting purposes. They're easily sized, and they are distinct in their attitudes, their media consumption, and their life-stage needs. That goes a long way!

The challenge, however, and why cohort targeting can be hard to use as the only lens for targeting, is that within a cohort, people are very likely to be behaviorally different with respect to a product category.

For instance, my brother and I are four years apart in age. We're both baby boomers by definition. However, we couldn't be more different in our preferences. We eat different foods and drink different beverages. While we both stream a great deal of content, what we watch is different.

Demographic Sub-Segments

Demographic sub-segments are descriptive characteristics that improve your understanding and the nuances of a segmentation and customer target. However, demographic sub-segments are not necessarily the perfect starting point, because they separate people based on external characteristics and not on how they think.

So, while sub-segments are correlated with some behaviors that enable the marketer to understand the target customer, marketing to a particular sub-segment (or micro-segment) can be tricky if you're not considering attitudes and needs, as well.

Income and Socioeconomic Status

Income and socioeconomic status(es) are pretty reliable predictors of buying power, and are excellent profiling variables. But not all of those potential customers in an income bracket think in the same way.

A composite variable like SES creates a tighter definition of a high-income, high-education customer, a smart target for some high-end luxury goods. Considered in combination with other variables—especially those that explore the more attitudinal side of the customer—SES will improve your understanding of those in each income strata.

Gender Identity

Like socioeconomic status, gender identity is a variable that you can use to quickly learn if there is genuinely a gender-dominant customer target group. Men and women do tend to approach purchasing brands differently with regards to the analysis they do and the factors that influence them.

In B2C, men and women share the same needs when searching for products to solve their problems. The cannabis category is a great example. Both men and women get anxiety. Both men and women are looking to solve the problem with a CBD product. Both may buy the same product. But their decision process is likely to be different.

Some brands can be single-gender focused. Obviously, there are single-gender categories where this makes perfect sense (e.g., feminine hygiene products or men's shaving products.) Most brand targeting, however, needs to be more inclusive.

Race and Ethnicity

When doing segmentation work and searching for the customers who are likely to be interested in your products, you need to be careful about how you think of race and ethnicity. Inclusivity and respect are fundamental to any communications but more important with regard to people of color and different ethnicities.

Race refers to the physical differences that groups and cultures consider socially significant. For example, people might identify their race as African American or Black, Asian, White, Native American, or Pacific Islander, or some other race. Race is a social construct that not everyone uses in the same way. Ethnicity refers to shared cultural characteristics such as language, ancestry, practices, and beliefs.

Over the years, study after study has pointed out how consumers of different under-represented sub-segments desire more representation from brands in advertising and communications— for brands to be more inclusive and reflect their identities. A survey commissioned by Facebook found that both Spanish-dominant and bilingual Hispanics tend to gravitate toward Spanish-language content online, both in terms of consumption and creation.[21]

A brand doesn't need to be progressive to be more inclusive in how they go to market, but segmenting a market simply based on race or ethnicity will be challenging unless you are specifically offering brands that are relevant only to that sub-segment.

Geodemographic: Birds of a Feather

Census tracts and blocks are sometimes used as targeting approaches for local retailers. That's because birds of a feather really do flock together. It has been demonstrated that people move into neighborhoods with people who share similar characteristics, including political ideology.

In June 2014, the Pew Research Center surveyed the political polarization of the American public.[22] They found that those with a conservative ideology tended to favor houses that were larger and farther apart, with schools and restaurants several miles away. Those with a more liberal ideological persuasion tended to favor more walkable communities.

The Obama campaign took this to the next level. He was one of the first elected officials to use this micro-segmentation strategy to reach voters with his message.

Retailers do something similar by looking at trade areas. Most chain stores and grocery retailers, when looking for new locations, look at the neighborhoods within a twenty-minute traveling distance to a proposed site. If the area resembles their target audience, then establishing a store there makes sense.

Micro-segmentation works and is a nice add to any targeting work you develop.

Behavioral Influence

"Change your thoughts, and you can change the world" is a famous quote attributed to Minister and Author Norman Vincent Peale. Changing the world isn't easy. And, likewise, it is tough to change the way people think and behave.

Usage

Segmenting on usage is excellent because it is easier to build on a behavior than to create a new one. All of the big consultancies (e.g., McKinsey, Bain, BCG) have their own way of looking at heavy user targeting. Some refer to it as the 80/20 rule, finding the 20-percent-or-so group of people who are 80 percent of your volume or revenue. Some only look at the super heavy users—the top 5 percent of people who represent the most revenue.

Understanding heavy users, those who interact with your product the most, will tell you a good deal of why they buy what they buy. They tend to become very familiar with a product, and rather than experiment with new products or services, they repurchase the same product. Targeting users by frequency of purchase and usage is easy as long as you have the data.

Segmenting based only on usage behavior isn't always the easiest to understand. Not all heavy users are alike. Even though heavy users buy the same product, they tend to come from different backgrounds. Including secondary variables will improve your understanding and the power of the segmentation. The wealth of data generated from online web browsing and purchasing both from company sources and third-party sources (e.g., credit card companies and mail lists) are phenomenal overlays that improve the depth of understanding behind usage.

A retail client of mine found that one category—shoes—was the most powerful in its ability to predict how much money a customer would spend in the entire store over a year. But what else they purchased and the messaging to which they responded varied dramatically.

Aside from the frequency of purchase and dollars spent on shoes, digging deeper into the attitudinal data provided a more robust segmentation and targets that were more actionable.

Attitudes/Psychographics

If demographics help explain the "who," then psychographics help explain the "why." To understand "the why behind the buy," consider customers' perceptions of themselves, their interest in new products, their perceptions of the category, and who they trust:

- Do they read reviews?
- Do they trust Instagram?
- Do they like to buy online vs. in-store?
- Do they usually not follow brands?
- Do they only read negative reviews?
- Do they trust testimonials?
- Do they spend on indulgences?

These are customer attitudes and not yet about the products.

- If, for instance, a customer considers themself an early adopter, then they become a great resource for beta testing new software.
- If, for instance, they don't perceive themselves as being a social person, don't ask them to advocate for your brands, because they won't do it well.

These attitudes are not about the societal perspectives that can be inferred by cohorts, but about personal ways of thinking and behaving that can only be revealed by probing more deeply into their self-perceptions.

Occasions and Missions

Occasion- or mission-based targeting was born out of a consumer goods way of looking at customers.

The day in the life of the customer starts in the morning and works its way to bedtime. Throughout the day, the customer has different needs for different products to support the day—to provide sustenance, to provide focus, to provide energy, and to aid productivity, to name a few.

If you were a beverage company, you'd offer juice or smoothies in the morning with perhaps a little caffeine. Later in the morning, a bit more caffeine. At lunchtime maybe, tea to go with food.

A simple eating occasion-based structure might look something like this:

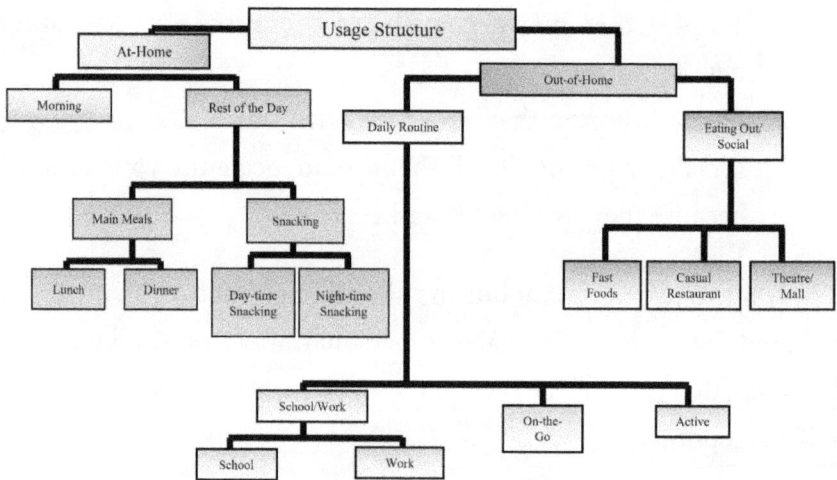

Usage Structure

At-Home
- Morning
- Rest of the Day
  - Main Meals
    - Lunch
    - Dinner
  - Snacking
    - Day-time Snacking
    - Night-time Snacking

Out-of-Home
- Daily Routine
  - School/Work
    - School
    - Work
  - On-the-Go
  - Active
- Eating Out/ Social
  - Fast Foods
  - Casual Restaurant
  - Theatre/ Mall

Retailers spend a great deal of time organizing their store around occasions because that is the way their customers think when they're shopping.

Targeting based on occasions alone can be challenging because of the variety of needs that may occur within an occasion. Combining occasions with other data to build a segmentation provides the who, what, why, and where of the buyer.

Needs and Problem Detection

Targeting based on customer pain points is perhaps the most actionable approach, because needs and problems are the motivations for which buyers seek solutions. People struggle with so much minutia in their lives that they try hacks to make their lives easier.

- Think about the precious time spent working with cloud-based computing. How easy is it to edit a document? Would you prefer Google Docs and DropBox for sharing documents? Or do you prefer the versatility of Microsoft Word?

- How about professional tax services vs. software? Money savings vs. time savings trade-offs?

- In the Pet Food world, the pain point of carrying heavy bags in and out of cars is significant, as is storing those same eighty-pound bags so that critters don't nibble at the bag corner.

- Think about the last time you had to wait in line for coffee early in the morning. Companies like Starbucks and Dunkin' Donuts offer mobile ordering, so you can order your coffee while in route and have it ready for you when you arrive. Skip the line. Save time. Waiting in line is a pain.

- People may seek beverages for energy or calming needs. Laptops may be purchased for lightweight or power needs.

- Consider the IT professional looking to share information across an organization, who needs increased storage or who needs access to faster and faster Wi-Fi speeds.

- Pain points embedded in aging are another such lens. Aging customers need easy-to-open bottles, packages that are easy to get from the store to the trunk of the car, and larger print on apps or software so they can be more productive and not have to work hard to engage with it. All of these are pain points.

Needs and problems are the most leverageable factors for segmentation and targeting, because people will act if you're solving their problems.

5. Fit for Purpose

A cross-category segmentation and targeting strategy for a broad portfolio is the best approach, but it is incredibly challenging to find something that fits every brand. Every solution will require a different approach.

- In the apparel story at the beginning of the chapter, age worked really well.

- The cube was an illustration used for how one client began to approach the multidimensionality of food service.

- For a lottery client, a blended attitudinal and socioeconomic model worked best.

- For a clothing retailer, a behavioral model based on dollars spent and categories shopped work best.

- For a phone maker, it involved identifying those with needs for using phones and providing them with the attention they required to retain their loyalty—before they switched.

- For a SaaS company, a blend of behavioral and attitudinal data worked the best. This approach allowed us to take advantage of the deep behavioral data collected from their user database.

Probably the most successful targeting work comes from bringing all of the elements together.

For Del Monte and Big Heart Pet Brands, a blended approach of all of the elements was incredibly powerful. For both of these portfolios, the best model combined the economics of socioeconomic status with lifestyle attitudes, behavioral data on purchasing, needs for using products, and brand affinity data. For both companies, it launched new approaches to media, innovation, marketing, and strategy.

6. ITRAC

I always recommend trying to collect a wide variety of data—to cast a wide net—so that when the time comes, you'll have the ability to look at the data any way you'll need to.

When I first joined PepsiCo, we were collecting consumption data using a mail survey. Mail surveys were an outdated technique and the data was showing signs of significant error.

For many reasons, but mainly to improve the quality of data, we embarked on a major re-engineering of the tracking data set. Using "hand-helds," we deployed a three-minute survey that would be filled out every time a person would take a drink.

The survey data included:

- Occasions

- Attitudes
- Brand ratings
- Who they were with
- Where they drank it
- The needs they were trying to solve

This data became the foundation for all our tracking data and the principle source to populate the cube.

7. Buyer Personas

Buyer personas are story-like representations of your customer targets. They help everyone intimately understand the customer and make it easier to tailor content to the specific needs, behaviors, and concerns of different groups.

A buyer persona is a one- or two-page profile that describes the target customers. Consider the profile of Healthy Holly. Sharing her profile helps everyone understand her and the people whom she represents. From the narrative, we understand who they are and what they care about. The profile page is followed by the data that supports the insights behind Holly's behavior.

The personas include a fictitious name that helps define the segment. The name could be as simple as "Holly" or as complex as "LOHAS" (which is an acronym for "Lifestyle of Health and Sustainability"). So, when you say, *"Meet Jane, she is the LOHAS customer,"* you would be able to remember who she is and what segment she represents.

Another one of McCullough's laws emphasizes the importance of the segment name.

"The name of the segment is almost as important as the segment itself."

Sometimes, people who are not that close to the work will have trouble remembering the details of a segment. Having a segment name that communicates its persona without ever having to look at the data makes the entire targeting segmentation portable from conversation to conversation.

Healthy Holly — 33%

Holly is a young mom with kids under 12. She and her husband both work and are struggling to make ends meet. They shop mainstream grocery, but try and buy organic whenever they can afford to. Passionate about health and well being, she loves to eat well and buys the best ingredients she can. Holly also has a dog which she treats as well as her husband!

WHO	• Younger marrieds with active lifestyles; in need of social acceptance, looking good, attractive, and indulging when possible. • Driven by their pursuit of happiness and their need to discover nature and reach spiritual balance.
HEALTH INVOLVEMENT	• Eating for a healthy life means enjoying healthy, tasty foods that fit with my lifestyle
CONVENIENCE NEEDS	• Stressed – Not a lot of time to prepare dinner • Needs healthy snacks in convenient Packaging

Another famous target name is "The Road Warrior," which represented the businessperson who traveled all the time—whether by planes, trains, or automobiles.

Then, narratives are created from the personas to describe the target segment. With Crashing the Culture and Hacking the Culture, actors performed skits so that those focused on the buyer journey (marketing, innovation, and sales functions) were able to get a complete understanding of the buyer.

7. The Bullseye

A good target segmentation should give you a bullseye target from which you can develop messaging, communications strategy, product development, marketing strategies (including pricing), and channel strategies.

The bullseye target has an aspirational component to it. Each ring outside that bullseye should find something in the bullseye message that will appeal to them as well. The spill-over, outside the target ring, broadens your addressable market without compromising the core target.

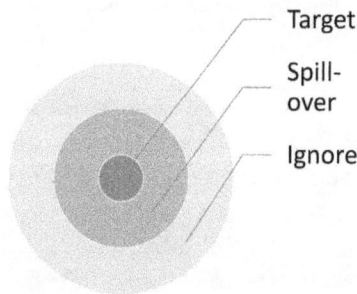

Target

Spill-over

Ignore

That's why advertising to boomers with a message meant for someone their age will be less effective than finding a more youthful message. The younger message is more aspirational and appealing to an aging segment. Boomers tend to be vain on top of that. They just don't like to think of themselves as aging, so they respond to more youthful messaging.

Don't take targeting for granted. Look at what you can do with a smart targeting approach:

- Tailoring products to meet the needs of your target audience
- Positioning and messaging to remain relevant
- Buying media and showing up where the target is spending time
- Pricing products, not only to be competitive but to fit the pocketbooks of your most-valued customers

"Creativity is intelligence having fun."
—Albert Einstein

CHAPTER 5

The North Star

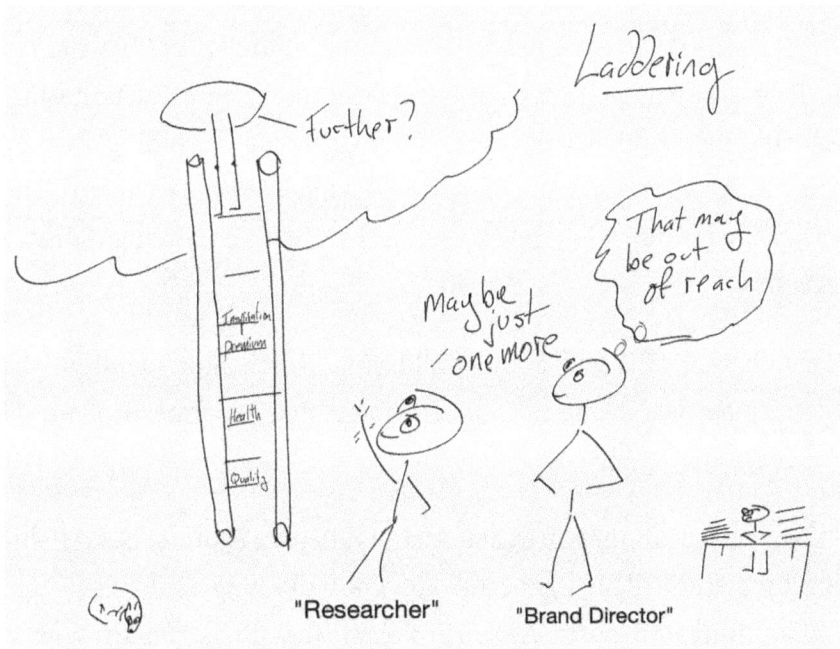

2001

In 2001, I was running strategic research for Pepsi. As part of that responsibility, I would work on select topics each year, preparing for strategic planning processes. My presentation usually kicked it off. It typically involved category usage, growth, macro trends, and the behavior of our key customer target segments. This year, we wanted to know how marketing spending was impacting the business. So, the presentation focused on the impact of those advertising dollars on revenue.

Pepsi had just spent a good deal of money on the *Joy of Cola* and *Joy of Pepsi* campaigns. In typical Pepsi fashion, high production value and big-name musicians were being deployed, including Britney Spears, Aretha Franklin, and the darling, Hallie Eisenberg. The campaigns were widely celebrated in the press and among industry execs.

This chapter will talk about building a North Star identity—the identity for which the brand stands and that separates it from all other brands.

When we talk about North Star identity, Pepsi's is pretty clear. Pepsi has been and will always be an expression of living a life of fun, joy, celebration, and music. An early slogan was, "Pepsi, for those who think young." So, when you think of Pepsi's identity, you think of some of the biggest names in music—from Michael and Janet Jackson to Aretha Franklin, David Bowie, Madonna, Ray Charles, Britney Spears, Shakira, Missy Elliot, and Beyoncé. The Pepsi brand is a cultural Zeitgeist. Pepsi stands for more than just a brand; it represents those who "think young" generation after generation.

For the advertising to break through and lift the brand above the category, generating incremental revenue, the branding and the advertising has to be exceptional.

The Britney Spears ad used iconic imagery from the Pepsi Cola sign from across the East River of Manhattan. It was pure Pepsi. Great music. Entertainment.

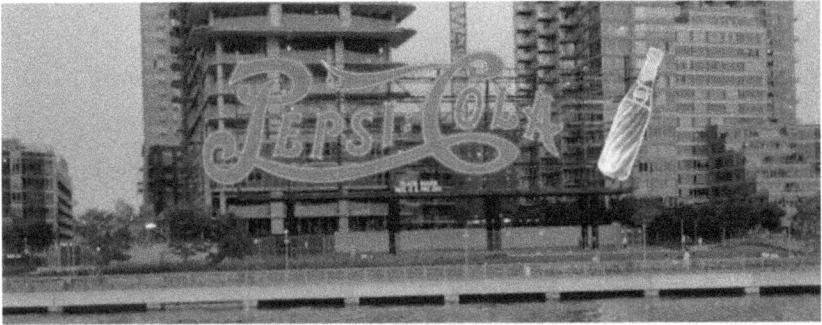

Reflective of the mood of the moment and coming off a not-so-optimistic "Generation Next" campaign that was a little on the dark side, the advertising reflected the generational desire for hope and optimism (something that Barack Obama would tap into). *Joy* was right in the sweet spot.

When the analysis was complete, it was clear that Pepsi had found something meaningful that resonated with customers, and drove incremental growth above the category.

2005

The longer you work in marketing, the more you appreciate the challenge of getting it right. Everyone has an opinion of what it takes to build a great brand and how it should be expressed. A VP of Media and Communications once said (and I paraphrase), "When it comes to advertising, everyone has an opinion about what I do, and I'm never right. Everyone always thinks they can do better."

1. The Promise of Purpose

Top-performing brands are built on ideals with higher-order purposes that transcend product. They are the promise and purpose of a company.

A mission is a promise. It is a stake in the ground about what is important to you and what you are trying to accomplish. The mission is the North Star for the company. Carefully crafted mission statements represent the collective mindset of the company. They align everyone in the organization to focus on one thing.[23]

- **Starbucks's mission** is to "Inspire and nurture the human spirit—one person, one cup, one neighborhood at a time."

- The **Big Heart Pet Company's mission** was to "Nurture the bonds between pets and the people who love them."

- **Nike's mission** is to "Bring Inspiration and Innovation to Every Athlete in the World."

- **Apple's mission** is "To bring the best user experience to its customers through its innovative hardware, software, and services."

- **Amy's Kitchen's mission** is "To provide delicious, organic, vegetarian prepared meals for people who appreciate good food but are often too busy to cook."

- **Warby Parker's mission** is "To offer designer eyewear at a revolutionary price while leading the way for socially conscious businesses."

- **Tesla's mission** is "To accelerate the world's transition to sustainable energy."

- **Salesforce's mission** is "To empower companies to connect with their customers in a whole new way."

Some mission statements are lofty, with a higher earthly purpose, like Tesla's or Nike's. Others are closer to the customer purpose, like Amy's Kitchen's and Starbucks. Neither is wrong.

Every department and every employee agrees to work within the mission as the singular purpose for existing. If a tough decision has to be made, look at whether or not it is consistent with the mission.

Many companies, like Kikoko, a women-owned Cannabis Tea company, have used their mission to explicitly lay out how they will work with others as part of the guiding principles (values). In Kikoko's case, its "six rules" include "... *we won't do business with people who are rude, condescending, disrespectful, flaky, patronizing, discriminatory, amoral ...*'" No Exceptions."[24]

Mission and brand identity have different reasons for being. The mission is the overarching statement about the company. The brand identity is how you want customers to perceive the brand. If the brand and the company are the same, the mission represents the principles against which the company will measure itself. The brand represents more about the outward expression of the brand (though this will get nuanced a little later in this chapter.) The brand identity is in service of supporting and delivering against the promise of the mission.

2. Brands Carry Their Own Meaning

When you hear brand names or see their logos, what do you think? For those that are well-established, there is instant recognition. Take brands like Pepsi, Apple, IBM, Levi's, Dove, Netflix, Google, Harley-Davidson. You know what they stand for, and knowing about them, you also know what their competitors stand for almost immediately.

Their identity has given the category meaning and shape. It reserves places for these brands in the minds of customers and places their competitors in a different space.

Brands help simplify customer choice. Strong brands, ones that have a solid positioning and identity, enable companies to focus resources, improve marketing effectiveness, and strengthen the culture behind their brand mission.

A strong identity aligns everyone behind a clear and unified description of the brand. When shared externally (e.g., agency partners) it will reinforce what the brand is and what it is not.

- The identity is the creative transformation of the brand that holds marketing activities together in a distinctive, inspiring, and cohesive way.

- It is a key differentiator for the brand that cuts across people and places and will stand the test of time.

- It creates a meaningful space in the hearts and minds of your customers.

A strong identity is the foundation of how you go to market, what channels you choose, and the entire marketing mix cascades from it. It is the reason *why* your audience would want to buy your brand *and not* from the competition.

3. Four Steps

World-class brands are distinctive, have rational appeal and emotional appeal, and have a clear, strong positioning.

There is a process that I use to bring all of the relevant pieces of information together to reveal the brand essence and build brand identity.

The steps to building a strong brand identity can be found in the public domain all over the internet, even on LinkedIn. On top of that, there are plenty of consultants who use their own proprietary tools that are either similar or more advanced. Some are drivers-based models, others are emotive models, and still others are neural models (and some combine all of those into one model.) They all do essentially the same thing, and I encourage you to learn about them.

But to stay in line with the purpose of this book, you should be able to do this simply. Here are the steps that I use for my clients.

1. Build out the brand pyramid.
2. Define the brand positioning.
3. Tell the brand story.
4. Develop guardrails.

4. Brand Pyramid

The Brand Pyramid is a simple tool to organize information in such a way that you can clearly see what the brand stands for and how it fits into the customer mindset.

What do your customers think? What do they need? To what message will they be receptive? How do you add value to their lives? What other products do they buy to serve those needs?

Starting from the very bottom, the pyramid begins with examining the category, then understanding who the customer is and what their needs are, then what benefits you offer, then the brand character and brand essence.

The bottom of the pyramid consists of facts, easily unearthed and assembled. The top of the pyramid consists of emotions born from those facts and then "laddered up" into the essence of what the brand means to its customers.

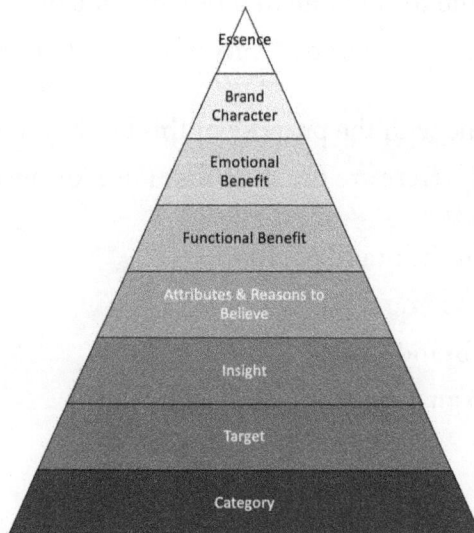

Category Framing

Death by a Thousand Bites

At Pepsi, for over a decade, I watched that master brand, the name on the door, slowly lose market share. But how? Pepsi had always been perfect for food accompaniment. Perfect for a quick pick-me-up (in fact, Diet Pepsi is the choice beverage for stand-up comic Marc Maron—to get pumped up for his shows). Perfect for a social occasion. Pepsi was perfect for so many occasions. And it had a distribution network that could only be matched by Coca-Cola.

Then slowly, bottled iced tea came into the meal accompaniment space, then energy drinks started to steal share in the pick-me-up space, and then water took its place in the social space (as well as many others.) All of a sudden, little by little, the brand share eroded—despite all that distribution power.

The moral of the story is to know how you're going to compete and with whom. If the brand is framed in a broad way, the competitive set is broad, and it might be difficult to find a space not already claimed by competition. Or, your brand might find itself in a situation like Pepsi's where there will be too many competitors to fend off. If it is framed up too narrowly, then the opportunity may not have scale to succeed.

Keep track of how the category changes and how your product fits into the category as it changes.

Customer Target

In the previous chapter, we discussed the way to identify the bullseye customer. Here we drop that definition into the next rung up on the brand pyramid. The customer target at the base of the pyramid reinforces to whom the brand is going to be marketed.

There is no need to restate the content of the previous chapter. But, if you're unsure, re-visit that chapter to make sure the customer bullseye is solid and clear.

Universal Truth

The next level of the brand pyramid is all about the core customer insight behind the brand. Some call it the unique selling proposition (USP). At Big Heart Pet Brands, it was called the central unifying idea. I like to think of this as the underlying universal truth that motivates customers. The universal truth is the core insight for why your brand exists in the minds of the customer. It is *the* launching point for your branding strategy. Identifying universal truths focuses on the benefits sought and why customers choose your brand over other brands.

For instance, one universal truth born from the seed of government distrust was that people were increasingly looking for corporations to step up and be active members of the community. People were looking for assistance, and for companies who were helping those in need. New businesses started to emerge whose fundamental idea was based on social responsibility. Toms Shoes is a perfect example of a company whose origin is based on the notion of giving back.

Today, nearly every Fortune 500 company has a community impact statement and an Office of Corporate Social Responsibility (CSR). Business is stepping up with more purpose- and mission-driven programs to fill in the gap where the government has not been able to. CSR initiatives have been shown to increase sales, employee productivity, and satisfaction. This universal truth was born out of a social movement and a desire for change.

Universal truths don't have to be about saving the world. In fact, universal truths are rarely that lofty. A universal truth can be about how customers feel about health and wellness, the lack of time to get things accomplished at work, or something more straightforward— like getting a cat to spend time with its parents.

Universal Truths should be tightly linked to and born from the category purpose and the target customer's needs.

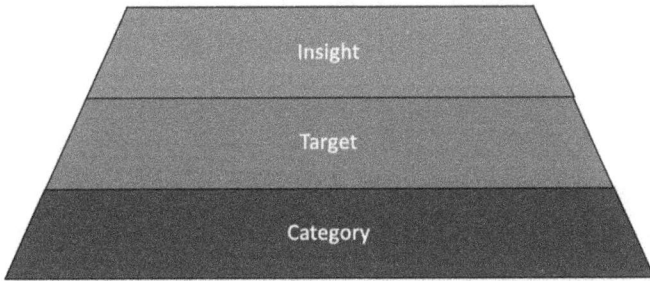

The health and wellness beverage category is crowded with a wide range of options. The category ranges from the genuinely healthy pro/prebiotic teas and kombuchas to the basic option of water and the indulgences of juices. A simplified bottom to the healthy beverages pyramid might look something like this:

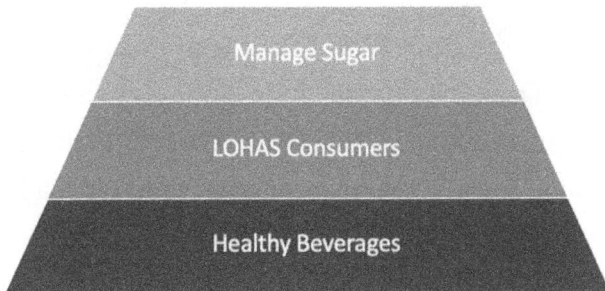

LOHAS customers look for healthy beverages to manage their sugar intake. They are looking for a "Lo-No" option. That is a beverage with the absence of sugar, calories, and unhealthy ingredients.

Universal truths come from engaging with your target customers. It can be easy to feel like you know what the customer wants without talking with them. It's important to check in with them to test those assumptions. Marketing research and insight reveal these truths. You can guess at them, but you can't know them unless you talk to your customers.

The in-depth work to reveal what is important to customers is the first step, not focus groups, which tend to wash out any meaningful depth. In-depth work helps to understand the pain points, solutions sought, and perceptions of other brands in the category (I repeat this often through this book because understanding these is the basis for being customer-centric.) These in-depths are usually cathartic for the client, the customer, and the researcher—worthy of the time and expense.

The learning generated in these sessions will promote new ideas that you will not have expected. Creative teams use this work as the fertile soil from which new work and new truths will emerge.

If the budget allows, market research should go beyond the qualitative work and involve quantitative work to size and validate the learning. True, everything done to that point will still be meaningful, but without validation, your work is still speculation. Without sizing, you will not know whether or not it will have scale.

The next rung up the ladder is examining the multi-dimensional benefits delivered by the brand and product. Laddering these up to the emotional benefits is next.

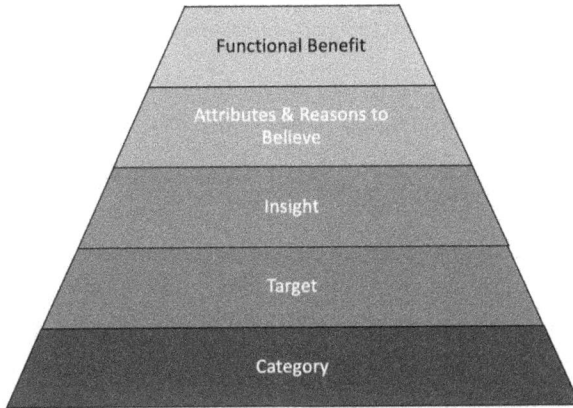

Attributes, Reasons to Believe, and Functional Benefits

Think of the grouping of attributes, reasons to believe (RTBs), and functional benefits as the rational facts and benefits delivered by the brand and product. For simplicity, I like to group these together and work with them as a whole. Feel free to break these down—it may make the process a little easier later on. But it's not necessary.

So, what does a product actually do? What are the attributes? What are the features? Where was it grown? What is it made of? How fast does it go? Those are the attributes and they ladder up to the functional benefits.

- In B2C marketing, like the food industry, it might be that a product keeps the users' sugar content lower, or, alternatively, is better tasting.

- In industrial B2B marketing, like IT Infrastructure and database software, it might be that the product is in the cloud or is faster or can handle more users.

- In B2C Finance, a functional benefit might be the integration of all your accounts. Many apps, banks, and brokerage firms offer that feature now.

- In B2B and B2C health care marketing, the functional benefit might be that the product makes it easier for employees to manage their health.

Why should anyone believe that a brand will fulfill their needs or solve their problems? RTBs are proof that your brand can deliver on its promise. These are the critical product attributes and features that are your proof points. If they are not there, then your brand promise will be hollow.

They provide the credibility and trust necessary for all other communications to be possible. Some brands just say they can deliver on the promise even if they can't. But few can get away with the lie, especially in this day of watchdog groups and demand for transparency. It is better to be safe and work with the truth.

RTBs can come from many areas of your business. They are both tangible and intangible:

The Tangible RTBs are rooted in functional aspects of the product, process, and data.

- Ingredients: Ingredients in products can be an RTB when they are rooted in the brand to project a level of quality or performance. Vitamin companies go to great lengths to source or create their own proprietary blends. Functional beverages like 5-hour Energy use their proprietary blends, Aside from CPG, you also see this in technology and electronics. For example, Sony and Dolby have leveraged each other's strengths to create award-winning products. The "Intel inside" campaign elevated the hardware brands that used the Intel chips, and elevated Intel imagery as an essential and exceptional product.

- Visual Communication Properties, Package Shapes, and Types: A package, shape, font, or logo becomes a reason to believe when it becomes a defining symbol for the company brand. This often occurs when something transcends into pop culture.

  Take, for example, Coca-Cola. It's "Hobble skirt" bottle shape debuted in 1915 and was one of the first glass containers ever to be patented based only on its shape. Salvador Dali, Marisol Escobar, Norman Rockwell, and Andy Warhol all helped turn the bottle into a pop culture icon.

  The same can be said for the Volkswagen Beetle "bug" shape—which has been used (albeit with some modifications) since its introduction in 1936.

- Production, Location, Process: Where a product is sourced from or how it is produced can be an RTB, especially when it is fundamental to the history of the origins of the product. A great example here is Evian water. According to company history, in 1789, during a walk, the Marquis of Lessert drank water from the Sainte Catherine spring on the land of M. Cachat. The Marquis, who was allegedly suffering from kidney and liver problems, claimed that the water from the spring cured his ailments.

- Process-based: In food marketing, the market force of healthy eating has manifested itself in the trend of "taking the bad out and leaving the good in." The "bad," of course, are things like saturated fats, excess carbohydrates, trans fats, and foods high in sodium. In advertising their removal, companies are assuring customers that the products still taste the same, or better.
  - o In a 1973 Super Bowl Ad, the slogan "Tastes Great. Less Filling" was born.
  - o In 1987, Dr. Pepper launched a diet version of its drink; the first advertisement stated, "Diet Dr. Pepper tastes more like regular Dr. Pepper."

- Testing & Claim-Based: If you have an advantage over your competition in some aspect, whether it's science-based or a customer-based preference, this is the kind of RTB you want to leverage.
  - o Pepsi made "The Pepsi Challenge"—a widely publicized taste test—a reason to believe.
  - o Think about how high-end restaurants and lodging establishments will tout their Michelin Star ratings, and consumer products will often promote a review by JD Power and Associates. Others rely on their Yelp ratings.
  - o There are claims like "Oral B removes 90% of plaque."

- PBS is the "most trusted source of news," according to an annual survey of American households.
- The sale of home improvement power tools is often associated with "the products used by professionals."

The Intangible RTBs are more focused on legacy, imagery, founder, and iconography. Some examples include:

- Legacy-based: If your reason to believe is that you've been around for 100 years, then that will translate well as a reason to believe that your grapevines or scotch is superior.
    - Johnny Walker whiskey describes its humble origins and recipe dating to 1819, beginning with the sale of the family farm.
    - Camper shoe company's origins trace back to 1877, when the grandfather of founder Lorenzo Fluxa bought his first sewing machine.
    - In the early 1980s, Smith Barney, a brokerage firm, was famous for ads that said, "We make money the old-fashioned way … we *earn* it."
    - Many brands have the seeds of an inspiring essence in their DNA and history, and that should be mined. But an old image can backfire if going up against younger, more progressive brands.

- Credentials and endorsements: Being associated with a "seal of approval" from trusted institutions or people is an excellent way to borrow credibility and trust.

Endorsements can come from users or experts, proven leadership, or credentialed professionals. For over 125 years, the American Dental Association has organized committees to study and approve toothpaste. A toothpaste that does not carry the ADA seal of approval might not sell as well as one that does.

While similar to testing-based, credentials are more about the origin of an endorsement.

Celebrity endorsements, particularly in the spirits business, have become a compelling reason to believe. Mila Kunis endorses Jim Beam and Ray Liotta endorses 1800 Tequila. Even in Tech, there are people like Ashton Kutcher, who endorses Lenovo computers. In Finance, Elizabeth Banks endorses State Street Banks.

- Company Origin: A unique origin like a tech company starting in a garage or basement of a founder, or the odd events that led to the creation of the business name.

In the case of Richard Branson, founder of Virgin Group, the name was suggested by one of Branson's early employees because they were all new at business.

In the case of Apple, Steve Jobs told biographer Walter Issacson that the name was chosen after Jobs said he was "on one of my fruitarian diets." He said he had just come back from an apple farm, and thought the name sounded "fun, spirited, and not intimidating."

The spirit of the company was in contrast to IBM and the "rebel" nature of the company that would later manifest itself in the "1984" advertisement and the "Think Different" campaign.

And, again, there is the example of Larry Page and Sergey Brin, who named their company Google, which was a derivation of googol, which is the numerical equivalent of a '1' followed by 100 zeros. The founders appreciated the name because they wanted to build a data-driven company that would aspire to "organize the world's information and make it universally accessible and useful."

- Product Serving Rituals: The way a product is poured or served. Blue Moon beer's trademark serving ritual is with an orange slice.

Brand Character

A person's character and personality are often defined by how they act and express themselves. And that's no different with a brand. The next level of the pyramid is Brand Character.

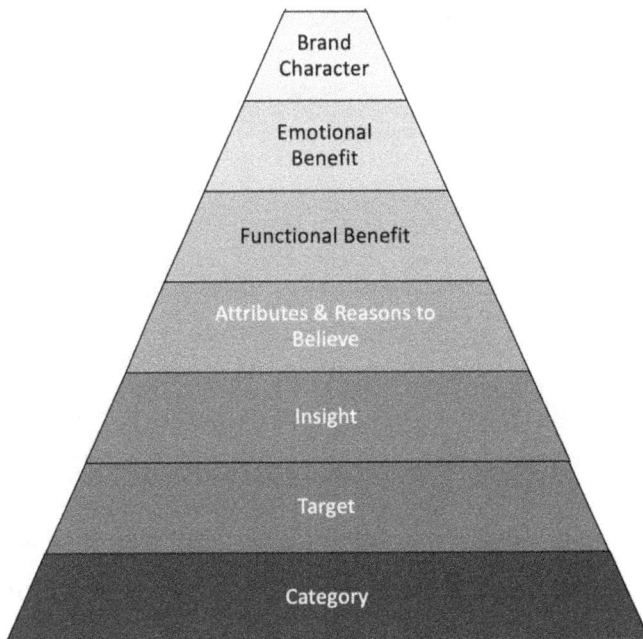

The brand's character is linked to the brand mission. It describes what the brand stands for, and how it behaves. Brand *Character* is the outward expression of the brand tone and belief system.

A brand's belief system is how it views the world, including political and social issues. It fuels its culture. Facebook's character and belief system are very different than that of Google's or Apples.

The brand's _personality_ traits are its tone, such as happy, youthful, or energetic. The personality should evoke a clear image of the brand as if it were a person. It should be engaging and inviting to the target audience.

Just as it's hard to change the perception of a politician's character once people get to know them, the same is often true for a brand. So, it is essential to establish character clearly through mission and purpose and take ownership, and to some extent, celebrate it.

Emotional Benefits

From the tangible, we now look at how a brand makes the customer feel? Attributes, RTBs, and functional benefits all ladder up to the emotional benefits of the product.

Emotional benefits are the visceral emotion or motivation that makes the customer interested in the product.

A specific benefit can fill both functional and emotional needs at the same time. Food is a great way to illustrate this.

Whereas a functional benefit might have been healthier foods, the emotional benefit might be that these foods make customers feel better or think they will live longer.

With the popularity of meatless burgers, some have pointed out the amounts of sodium and saturated fat in plant-based burgers as being just as unhealthy as in traditional burgers

A plant-based meat substitute may make the customer happier because less meat is slaughtered and the products are help saving the planet. The emotional benefit is less about being healthy and more about a better environment.

In the case of B2B marketing, security might ladder up to trust. Speed might ladder up to more time to perform other tasks.

In B2B Finance, budget management ladders up to peace of mind and self-reliance.

Emotional benefits are the inspirational building blocks for the brand identity in every case.

Differentiation

As you climb the pyramid, the benefits you choose matter more if they're unique. Even though you may have too many to count, look for key areas of differentiation.

"A Sea of Sameness" within a category is a common hurdle many need to overcome. In commodity categories, there is very little benefit differentiation between brands. Instead, benefits become table stakes. Safety in air travel, living longer in the pet food category, and quality of life in health insurance are examples of table stakes benefits that most brands can claim. These are necessary to compete, just not differentiating.

To create unique positioning, you need to find features and benefits that make your brand different—better. It only matters if it matters to the customer.

To simplify, you should ask the following questions about the benefits you want to convey to the customer:

- Are they motivating?
- Are they relevant?
- Do they resolve a pain point?
- Are they differentiating?
- Can you actually deliver on the promise?
- Do they connect to the core universal truth?

If you can answer "yes" to most of these questions, then these emotional benefits add to the foundation of your brand positioning. If not, then set them aside and revisit them later.

Essence

At the top of the pyramid is where it all comes together. The essence is what the brand stands for in the hearts and minds of the target.

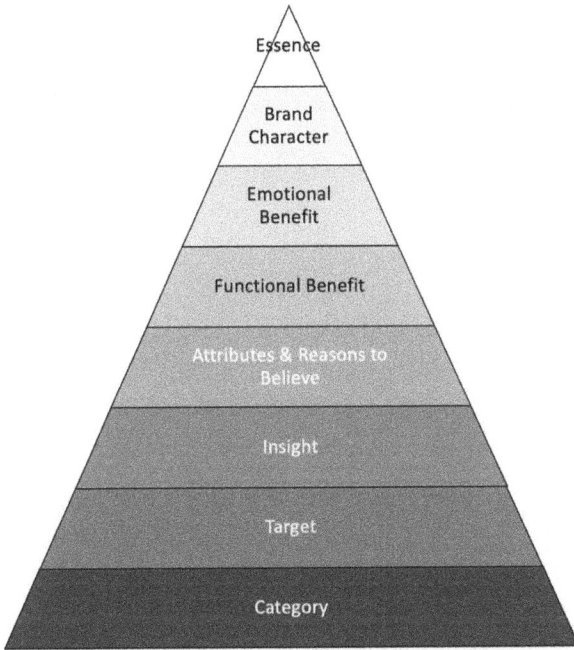

Essence sums up how the brand connects emotionally with the customer. It distills the brand down to the single notion that lies at the heart of the brand and the very core of its competitive advantage.

The features of a brand, or its RTBs (e.g., lightweight, fast, or blue), are more *tangible*. They're easy to sense, describe, measure, and compare. The character represents values and beliefs. The essence should be palpable and captured in just a few words. Its expression should be so compelling that only a few words are needed *because it is felt*.

An alternative island alcoholic beverage worked with me to build its brand pyramid. A near-final draft looked like the one above. The essence, "Everyone has a little bit of the islands in them," is a bit wordy for my tastes, but captures the heart and soul of the brand. They are committed to an authentic island life providing a lightweight celebratory alcoholic beverage to compete with beer, cider, and other low-alcohol alternatives.

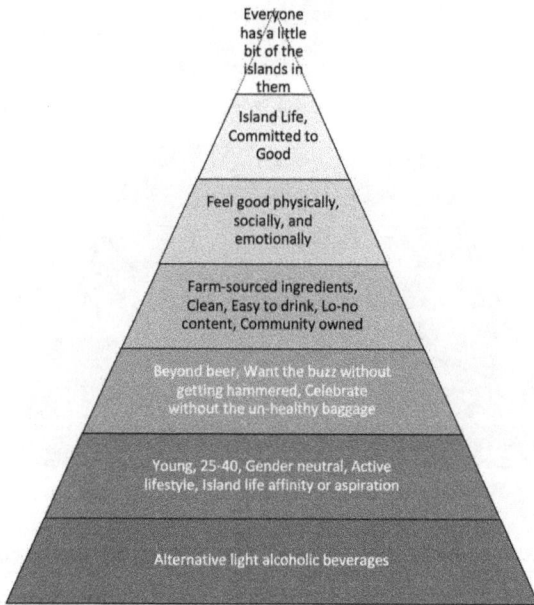

For this company, the pyramid is the perfect expression of their who they are, what they stand for, and what they value.

A brand pyramid can also be built for nonprofits as well. I like to devote some of my time assisting charity organizations that need help with their mission and strategy. Below is a concatenated pyramid for The Friends of The Inyo (National Forest).

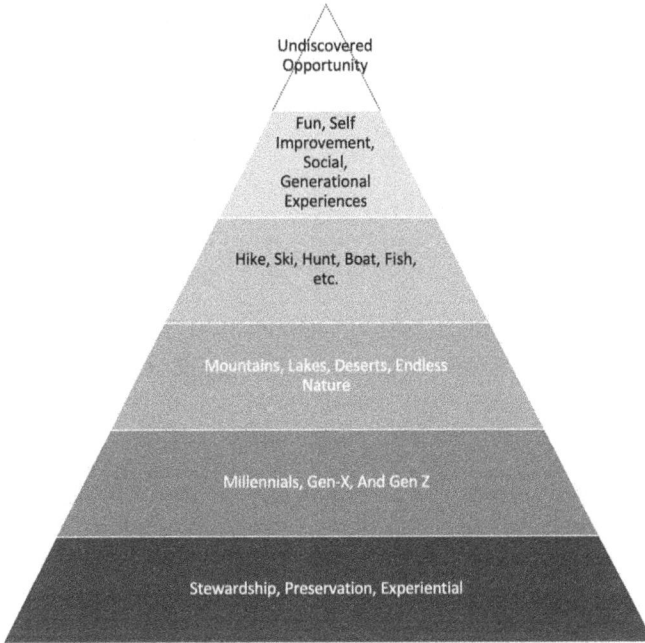

Undiscovered Opportunity

Fun, Self Improvement, Social, Generational Experiences

Hike, Ski, Hunt, Boat, Fish, etc.

Mountains, Lakes, Deserts, Endless Nature

Millennials, Gen-X, And Gen Z

Stewardship, Preservation, Experiential

6. Mapping

A valuable step in confirming how well you've done in creating your brand identity and differentiation from the competition is to spend some time to create a simple perceptual map.

Some mathematical models will do this if you've collected the data in advance. I find the easiest, and most generally reliable, is correspondence analysis. However, for this step, I think it would be safe to use whatever data you have at hand to map out the brand space.

Here's a simple map with the most straightforward labels possible. But what it clearly does is illustrate the identity of the brands and their separation from each other pretty quickly. When doing a validation of a brand's identity against the competition, be sure there is enough separation on the key attributes and benefits that drive the category.

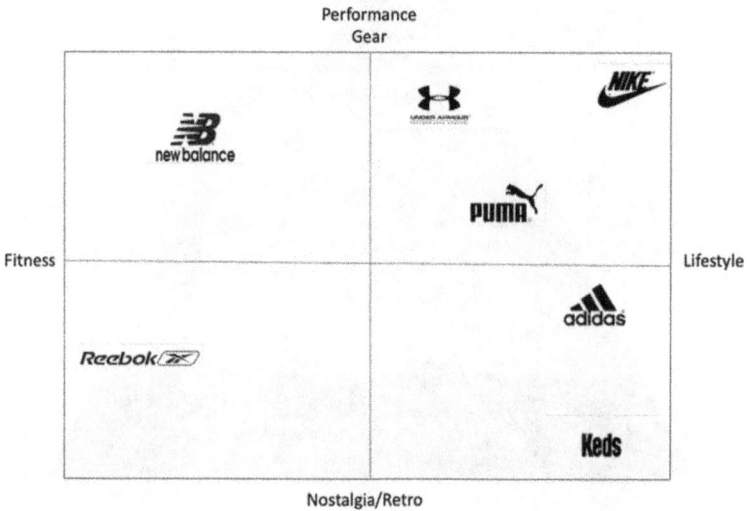

Do this with data preferably, but definitely do it so that you can visually see if you've done a good job in creating separation between brands.

7. Articulating the Essence

The positioning statement is the articulation of all the work done so far—from the mission all the way through to the essence.

Building the positioning statement is part formula and part art. It is the mechanism by which you start bringing together everything you have worked on to date. The who, the what, and the why come together in your positioning statement.

The Positioning Statement Formula

Generally, the formula for a positioning statement has the following elements:

- Target audience
- Category
- Functional benefits
- Reasons to believe
- Emotional benefits

The positioning statement should look something like this:

- For *(target audience),*
- Brand X is the *(category name)*
- that provides *(differentiating list of functional benefits).*
- Only Brand X has *(these key reasons to believe).*
- Brand X is the only brand that can provide *(most motivating emotional benefits).*

Stop here and think about this for a long second. Look at the components. It seems obvious now, right? You know your category and competitors. You have identified the customer and their needs. You have built a brand with the functional benefits that meet those needs that are different from your competition. You have the necessary proof points as to why you can deliver on the benefits. *And,* you have a message that communicates it. There you go—you've built the fundamental brand expression from the bottom up.

The benefit of the positioning statement is that it is the tool by which you build the creative, inform media buys, and build messaging. The positioning statement ensures that your entire organization knows who it is—and that it aligns with the company mission. Its purpose is to make sure that you have a clear and compelling story.

The island beverage might look something like the following:

> For the young-at-heart millennial (25-40) who has island life in their hearts—black sand beaches, island farms, mountains rising from the ocean, an active and celebratory chill lifestyle *(Target)*

> Brand X encourages you to celebrate without the "unhealthy baggage" of artificial ingredients and makes it easier to enjoy yourself. *(point of difference and functional benefit)*

> Brand X is great tasting, clean, uniquely flavored, and easy to drink without the "cloying" sweetness of artificial ingredients or high-calorie content. And it comes from the award-winning, authentic, and only community-owned Brand X. *(reasons to believe)*

> Celebrate island life, and feel good while doing good. *(emotional benefit)*

> Brand X. Everyone can have a little piece of island life.

8. Storytelling

All brands should tell their story. Not just the story that they have in the About section of their website, but the *emotional* story about what the brand believes in and why it exists. It is creative, and includes the mission, the culture, the essence, and the positioning.

Telling a compelling brand story can become the brand manifesto.

- It elevates the passion and emotion of your positioning statement to an inspiring narrative.
- It represents the guiding principles and a compass for employees to think and act in a way that delivers the brand's purpose or a company's mission.
- It takes into consideration the company's values, beliefs, and personality.
- It is inspirational, but grounded; authentic and emotional.

Here are some outstanding examples of manifestos[25].

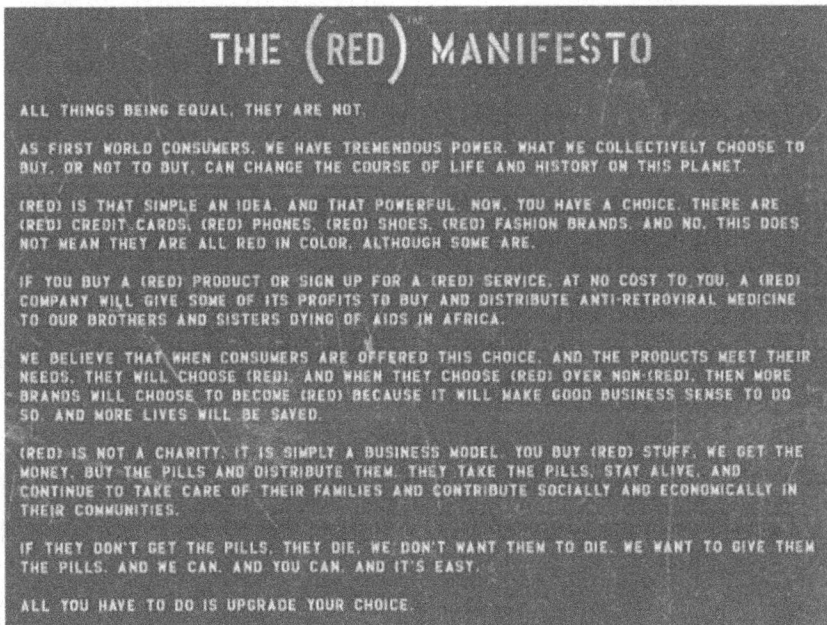

THE (RED) MANIFESTO

ALL THINGS BEING EQUAL, THEY ARE NOT.

AS FIRST WORLD CONSUMERS, WE HAVE TREMENDOUS POWER. WHAT WE COLLECTIVELY CHOOSE TO BUY, OR NOT TO BUY, CAN CHANGE THE COURSE OF LIFE AND HISTORY ON THIS PLANET.

(RED) IS THAT SIMPLE AN IDEA. AND THAT POWERFUL. NOW, YOU HAVE A CHOICE. THERE ARE (RED) CREDIT CARDS, (RED) PHONES, (RED) SHOES, (RED) FASHION BRANDS. AND NO, THIS DOES NOT MEAN THEY ARE ALL RED IN COLOR, ALTHOUGH SOME ARE.

IF YOU BUY A (RED) PRODUCT OR SIGN UP FOR A (RED) SERVICE, AT NO COST TO YOU, A (RED) COMPANY WILL GIVE SOME OF ITS PROFITS TO BUY AND DISTRIBUTE ANTI-RETROVIRAL MEDICINE TO OUR BROTHERS AND SISTERS DYING OF AIDS IN AFRICA.

WE BELIEVE THAT WHEN CONSUMERS ARE OFFERED THIS CHOICE, AND THE PRODUCTS MEET THEIR NEEDS, THEY WILL CHOOSE (RED). AND WHEN THEY CHOOSE (RED) OVER NON-(RED), THEN MORE BRANDS WILL CHOOSE TO BECOME (RED) BECAUSE IT WILL MAKE GOOD BUSINESS SENSE TO DO SO. AND MORE LIVES WILL BE SAVED.

(RED) IS NOT A CHARITY. IT IS SIMPLY A BUSINESS MODEL. YOU BUY (RED) STUFF. WE GET THE MONEY, BUY THE PILLS AND DISTRIBUTE THEM. THEY TAKE THE PILLS, STAY ALIVE, AND CONTINUE TO TAKE CARE OF THEIR FAMILIES AND CONTRIBUTE SOCIALLY AND ECONOMICALLY IN THEIR COMMUNITIES.

IF THEY DON'T GET THE PILLS, THEY DIE. WE DON'T WANT THEM TO DIE. WE WANT TO GIVE THEM THE PILLS. AND WE CAN. AND YOU CAN. AND IT'S EASY.

ALL YOU HAVE TO DO IS UPGRADE YOUR CHOICE.

"Here's to the crazy ones. The misfits. The rebels. The trouble-makers. The round pegs in the square holes. The ones who see things differently. They're not fond of rules, and they have no respect for the status-quo. You can quote them, disagree with them, glorify, or vilify them. But the only thing you can't do is ignore them. Because they change things. They push the human race forward. And while some may see them as the crazy ones, we see genius. Because the people who are crazy enough to think they can change the world, are the ones who do."

9. Brand Guardrails: Be Mindful of Swim Lanes

Brand guardrails put boundaries around what the brand is and is not supposed to represent. Using guardrails informs decision making and ensures brand consistency.

When developing guardrails, imagine what the future might look like for the brand. What feels like the brand, what doesn't? What would be in scope, what would be out of scope? Set the parameters for shaping the future of the brand. This should be revisited as the brand grows and develops new equities and may need to adjust to new market dynamics. Guardrails are the only thing set down that guide what you think your brand should be in 6, 12, 18, 24, and 48 months ahead.

Typically, you think about things like values, attributes, audience, and needs. But some brands' guardrails are more tactical by looking across the marketing mix (i.e., package design, product formulas, innovation).

There are many unknowns, and brand guardrails help make decisions easier by identifying those elements of the brand that must always be present and what elements can be left behind.

10. Art and Science

Building a brand identity is a blend of art and science. The science is the data and the insight you draw upon to fuel the art and creativity. There are some amazingly creative people out there who have had a great deal of success with only a little data at hand.

A start-up has very few resources. The founder has their vision. The ones who are most successful, however, are the ones who are building their identity with the customer front and center.

The more prominent companies often are at risk of thinking they have everything under control and that little needs to be done to create or nurture an identity. Nothing could be farther from the truth. It takes monitoring, learning, and staying on top of the market. Take care of the brand, and it will take care of you.

"Nothing great was ever achieved without enthusiasm."
—**Ralph Waldo Emerson**

CHAPTER 6

Tactics in Search of a Strategy

1998

Once upon a time, an "anointed" executive hired to run Frito Lay marketing said that trained monkeys could do market research.

Nothing could be farther from the truth. Brand marketers don't need to know market research. Market researchers, on the other hand, need to know both marketing, and marketing research. They need to know what their client partners are going through and how to help them.

2009

It's annual planning time. I've been with the company for about eight months now, and this is my first annual planning session.

We're all sitting in a big conference room at an off-site in a hotel along the beach. It's beautiful outside. We can see the ocean. We're inside, but there is the promise of golf later on—just a horrible idea considering the difficulty of the golf course. Such is the promise of this off-site.

As is always the case, the CEO sits at the head of a substantial U-shaped table. Probably fifteen Directors and VP's of Marketing, Sales, Finance, and Operations sit down the long sides of each part of the table.

We each have a book full of data and plans, color coded and with several appendices. The heads of the brands are presenting their plans for the coming year. As the day wears on, it dawns on me: There is no relevant customer information. The discussion is largely focused on finance and operating margins. The innovation strategy is mostly a list of line extensions. And, for the lack of solid insight, most would eventually fail when they hit the market months later.

Tactics in search of a strategy means there are no central objectives—just tactics without focus. As was the case in this meeting, there was the illusion of strategy. The forms were filled out, boxes were checked, backroom alignment attained, and decks were loaded with supporting charts and text.

Ultimately, the CEO doubted everything. In hindsight, it's easy to see why. Where was the foundational understanding of the customer?

The meeting was interminably long. Each tactic was scrutinized in search of a strategy or objective that held it together. If the strategy wasn't there, it was back to the drawing board to create a new approach or figure out how to back into one.

I realized that to be successful, we would need to change our narrative—to genuinely focus on understanding our market and our target customer. I always knew this, but this off-site crystalized that need.

Everything we did from then on led us to fact-based, insight-driven knowledge to drive strategy.

The golf was as expected. It was a beautiful day in the sun, spent struggling to find golf balls in tall grass, sand, and water.

1. Stratēgia

Strategy comes from the Greek *stratēgia*, meaning "generalship": a plan of action or policy designed to achieve a major or overall aim.[26] Marketing strategy is the marketing plan of action that includes the tactics that will help achieve that plan.

Strategy is not a gut call. Strategy is based on sound thinking. It is based on what you know about trends, the customer, the environment, the competition, organizational capabilities, the brands in the portfolio, supply chain, operational complexities, and sales capabilities.

"Getting it right" is about gathering all the work performed every day—the data collected, the conversations, the articles, the trends, in-market performance, targeting, positioning— everything. Strategy should be created from the insights drawn from all these aspects of the business. The fundamentals of insight-based marketing strategy require a knowledge base like the one below.

Fundamentals of Insight-Based Marketing Strategy

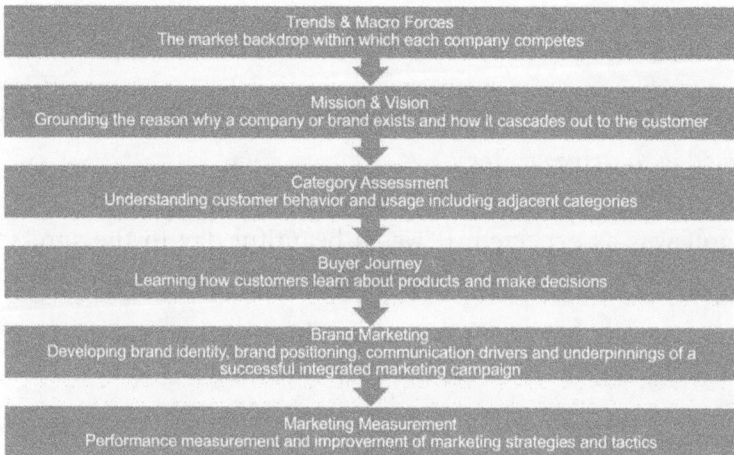

Trends & Macro Forces
The market backdrop within which each company competes

Mission & Vision
Grounding the reason why a company or brand exists and how it cascades out to the customer

Category Assessment
Understanding customer behavior and usage including adjacent categories

Buyer Journey
Learning how customers learn about products and make decisions

Brand Marketing
Developing brand identity, brand positioning, communication drivers and underpinnings of a successful integrated marketing campaign

Marketing Measurement
Performance measurement and improvement of marketing strategies and tactics

It is hard to pull all of this together without providing structure for it. To that end, the following pages illustrate how to build insight-based strategies from robust data structures and turn them into plans.

The best marketing strategy is informed by building a fact base focused on marketing goals or objectives. The objective could be something like:

- Improving brand revenue
- Innovating to refresh products
- Increasing the breadth of the portfolio
- De-scaling competition
- Improving brand equity

2. Taking Stock

In business school, we are taught to how to conduct a SWOT analysis—a 2x2 matrix where you take stock of your strengths, weaknesses, opportunities, and threats.

I have modified the SWOT slightly. Instead of the opportunities in a traditional SWOT, I suggest amplifiers.

- Strengths are positive, internal factors that affect how the business performs.
- Amplifiers, like opportunities, are the positive external factors (not within your control) that will affect the business. Amplifiers are those specific opportunities that provide the fuel to take the fullest advantage of both the opportunity and your strengths.

- Weaknesses are the negative, internal factors;
- Threats are the negative, external factors that are outside of your control.

I have found that in a normal SWOT, some opportunities are merely descriptive and not actionable. Amplifiers should act as multipliers for strengths when building a strategy.

SWAT

The SWAT analysis is relatively easy to create. Though any individual can do it, pairing the creative with the analytical sides of a team will increase the odds of coming up with a successful strategy. The analytical team comes with known data and objectivity; the marketer comes with the objective in mind, the brand stewardship, and the authority to act.

Strengths

Strengths are what you do best relative to your competitors. They are under your control to address and manage. Ask yourself these questions:

- What do we do well?
- What do we do better than anyone else?
- What is our competitive advantage?
- What resources do we have at our disposal?
- What advantages do our employees give us?
- What valuable assets does our company have?

You should do your best to probe deeply. Consider the strengths under your control, including:

- Brand and corporate reputation
- Databases/customers
- Capabilities
- On-trend practices
- Insights and research
- Talent
- Partnerships
- Intellectual property

Amplifiers

Think of Amplifiers as vital external forces that will increase the impact of your strengths. The amplifier is an accelerant—not something that just exists, but something that can be used as fuel. You don't own it, but you can take advantage of it.

Think about all the market forces and possibilities outlined earlier. For instance, you can't control age, but it can represent an opportunity. Age is only an amplifier if it provides you with momentum in the market place. You can't control the bifurcation of wealth, but you leverage that insight if it gives you the momentum to drive a value/premium brand strategy.

An amplifier, like marketing technology, can really propel a brand to reach more customers. In finance, technology changed the way Sofi, Credit Karma, and Nerd Wallet all were able to do business. Those weren't just gaps in the market, they were a combination of consumer need, company strength, and technology to accelerate the growth of that category.

Other questions you might pursue:

- Is the market changing favorably? How is it changing? Are new products entering the market and opening space for innovation?
- What potential technology changes could help business?
- Is the current economy going to affect us positively?
- What ideas have we not yet pursued?
- What new customers are becoming available?

Weaknesses

Weaknesses are in your control to address and manage, but they get in the way of what you can accomplish. Although they may be difficult to change, they should be within your control:

- What do our competitors do better than us?
- What disadvantages does our team carry?
- What is holding us back?
- Which resources are we lacking?
- What could we improve?

Threats

A threat is any key external force that can adversely affect your brand. And, like opportunities and amplifiers, many threats are born from market forces.

- What new players in the market could threaten your business?
- What industry-changing events could negatively impact your business?
- What does your supply chain look like?

- Are regulations changing in a way that could hurt your business?

Illustrations

In the illustrations that follow, you will find a SWAT Analysis for a fictitious traditional "too big to fail" financial institution that is trying to determine how it should respond to the growing threat of losing market share to Financial Technology (FinTech) start-ups.

The company finds itself with a strong brand and deep knowledge of the market. On top of that, they have proprietary tech that they can use to their advantage. The amplifiers are the momentum of technology in the category, and the willingness of younger consumers to adopt it, shows promise.

Strengths	Amplifiers
• A big company with a legacy and knowledge base of talented employees • Strong brand • A large customer base that provides a wealth of insights • Proprietary technology	• The potent popularity and customer interest in FinTech help all market players. • Deregulation of financial services creates new possibilities for new financial products and services. • Younger audiences are driving adoption through the use of new tech.
Weaknesses	Threats
• Competitive FinTech firms have more appeal to the younger millennial crowd. • Competition gaining market share • Competitors compete in more than one vertical. • Understaffed • Poorly funded • Weak margin structure	• Technology advances have made existing product delivery formats outdated. • Banking regulations have flexed, creating more room for competition.

On the downside, the company is poorly resourced and at a competitive disadvantage. There also looks to be some regulatory tailwinds for competitors to ride.

Here's another example using a fictitious CPG beverage and snack company.

This company has a strong brand with a loyal customer base. They're on trend with healthy ingredients and sustainable packaging. The two main amplifiers are the unmet needs in the category, and a growing distribution network—even a supply chain to support it.

Their weaknesses and threats center mainly around an unbalanced portfolio, competitive M&A activity, and a marketplace that is too crowded to support a lot of innovation

Strengths	Amplifier
• Strong brand imagery • A customer knowledge base that provides a wealth of insights • Healthy ingredients • Sustainable packaging • Deep innovation bench strength and product development • Large market share • Deep customer loyalty	• Growing marketplace leaves gaps in unfulfilled customer needs. • A new distribution network to improve access to healthy products • The new supply chain for exotic ingredients • New manufacturing technique changes the way products are packaged.
Weaknesses	Threats
• Unbalanced portfolio • M&A skill set weak	• The market is very crowded with existing products. • Limited sourcing capability • Competition M&A has been aggressive.

3. Strategy Development

After taking stock and summarizing the key insights, it makes sense to start building strategy by turning strengths and amplifiers into actionable plans. Trying to correct weaknesses is not a strategy. Fixing weaknesses is better addressed with an internal initiative.

So, strategy development starts with the insights you have at hand.

- What are you learning?
- Does that set of data point you in a particular direction?
- Can you say, "Oh, I learned something by combining this set of data."
- What do these facts and the insights help you decide?
- How important is it? What can you draw from it that you can act upon?

The data is your foundation from which you gain insight. Insights are not the data, but what the data means (remember the sports drink example in Chapter 2?). They provide you with a moment of clarity. With a little bit of creative thinking, you should be able to say to yourself, "Oh, this means something, I can use this." These insights become the launching point for building a marketing strategy.

Then pare down to only the top of the SWAT. Look for those areas where seeds of a strategy can be born. In the CPG case,

Strengths	Amplifiers	Implications
• Strong brand imagery • A customer base that provides a wealth of insights • Access to healthy ingredients • Deep innovation bench strength and product development • Deep pockets	• Category still growing • Growing marketplace leaves gaps in unfulfilled customer needs. • New distribution network to improve access to healthy products	• Take advantage of unserved needs. • Introduce new premium products. • Leverage access to ingredients and a new network.

Then,

Strengths	Amplifiers	Implication	Strategies
• Access to healthy ingredients • Deep innovation bench strength and product development	• Growing marketplace leaves gaps in unfulfilled customer needs. • New supply chain represents exotic ingredients. • New distribution network to improve access to healthy products	• Take advantage of unserved needs.	• Launch new healthy line of products to serve unmet customer needs.

Or,

Strengths	Amplifiers	Implication	Strategies
• Large market share • Deep pockets	• Category still growing	• Spend "into the market" to support the base brand.	• Drive loyalty among existing customers.

Strategy Sprints

Strategy sprints are designed to solve the problem of work sessions where people like to talk, posture, and generally be unproductive for several days. Instead, strategy sprints are short, focused, collaborative brainstorming work sessions. They have a specific outcome and follow-up. In a strategy sprint, people come to engage with each other. There is focus, ownership, and accountability.

While the overall strategy process can take time, a sprint is an easy, quick way to "get it right" and build strategy (and then plans).

Sprint Considerations

Here are some of the areas that should be considered for discussion. You'll most likely fall short. Don't go crazy—get what you need out of the sprint.

- Insights & research
- Marketing oversight
- Integrated marketing
- Digital marketing
- Content development & publishing
- Growth/growth hacking
- Innovation

If you are a start-up or a small team, likely there will be three of you in the room. Maybe only one! But it doesn't change the fact that you will need to consider these areas.

Once you start filling out the SWAT, be careful not to recycle myths. One of the most common mistakes, for whatever reason, is to think of yourself as the customer. The United States (and the world) is so diverse that keeping that view is, more often than not, misguided.

Use the data—not your gut. You're not trying to select only the data that proves yourself right. You're trying to makes sure that, objectively, the data points you in the right direction.

If you don't know something, put it in the proverbial parking lot, try to find the data, or consider it a risk. Then pare it down to things that matter.

Also, there are no formulas. While it is a quasi-plug-'n-play exercise, there will be no substitute for agile thinking. Best to consider all angles and then start whittling down. Some of these will take your weaknesses into account—but they will not be designed to fix them. If regulation is coming to restrict what you can do—like in cannabis, where it is tightly regulated what you can and cannot say—you will need to consider them as boundaries, but not the strategy itself.

Execution & Leadership

Strategy development can't be led by committee. It requires ownership, a clear leader, and vision.

As the owner, you need to consider many perspectives with a laser focus on how they are addressing an objective. It has to be cross-functional in nature to make sure that you are entertaining as many perspectives as needed.

The best analogy is one of the head coach of a football team. The head coach has to consider the offense, the defense, and special teams, and within each, there is the quarterback coach, the line coach, the cornerback coach, trainers, and so on.

As you build out the strategic blueprint, you will need to have all the necessary angles considered without compromising focus and execution.

4. Strategy Blueprint

This is where you turn your SWAT into something that resembles a blueprint. What goals are you going to establish? How are you going to track them, and what will you consider success?

The strategic blueprint is what you are going to do, and how you are going to do it. It is the plan that aligns with the strategies that you've built from the SWAT analysis.

It is essential to create strategies and tactics that can be tracked and measured—so goals cannot be overlooked. When in doubt, look to the advice of legendary management guru Peter Drucker, who said, "What gets measured gets managed."

When your strategy is grounded in data, facts that are measurable and trackable, it will give you a target to shoot for. It will allow you to be as creative as possible to achieve those targets.

The Objective-Strategy-Measures (OSM) chart below takes your worksheet and organizes it for action.

For each objective, describe the strategies and how you will measure success from those strategies. Earlier in this chapter, we described a SWAT analysis for a fictitious traditional "too big to fail" financial institution.

Here is what this might look like when developed further:

Objective

(Business need)

- Increase market share.
- Maintain relevance.

Strategies

(Sourced from Strengths and Amplifiers)

- Increase brand strength to get greater share of mind.
- Build or acquire new technologies (mobile, peer to peer) that can deliver the product in new ways.
- Attack new product verticals focused on meeting the needs of younger target markets.

Tactics

(Built from strategies)

- Advertise where millennials mostly consume media, such as YouTube and Instagram.
- Build an app product development team and recruit from experienced existing competitors.

Measures

(Quantifying the strategy)

- Gather favorable product reviews in publications that appeal to your target audience. Be recognized.
- Have the most-installed, highest-rated app in your category in the AppStore.

As you start executing your strategy, if you encounter something that isn't working, ask yourself: *Is it the strategy or the tactic that needs to change?*

These questions can be answered when you tie their performance back to metrics. What are you trying to achieve? Drive awareness? Gain household penetration? Increase loyalty? Increase advocacy? Add lifetime value? Think about what you are trying to affect.

If you are tracking the right metrics with the appropriate frequency (e.g., slow-moving industries may not need hourly updates) and if your tactics aren't working—pivot! Change the tactics. If you've done the right work, then a successful strategy will support a pivot.

Blindsided: Regulations

Industries face regulatory pressure all the time. One estimate puts the cost of regulatory compliance at nearly $2 trillion a year in the United States. Some industries, like the food industry, are particularly sensitive to regulation, especially when it comes to product labeling. In my home state of California, regulators are constantly changing the packaging requirements for cannabis products. And every change means the prior packaging must be destroyed. One cannabis entrepreneur located in Sonoma county was recently interviewed and remarked, "I know so many companies that have warehouses of packaging that, because the regulations changed, are just a loss… There's a lot you have to fit on a small package, so it's hard to put it all together in a way that actually looks good to the customer and keeps your brand looking nice." Product labeling causes a lot of pain, especially when every word is scrutinized.

5. Cascading Strategy

Throughout the first part of the book, I outlined how to identify the elements necessary to get the product-market fit right. This chapter outlined a process to complete a situation analysis and strategic blueprint.

Product-market fit gives you the foundation, the situation analysis brings it all together, and the strategic blueprint provides you with a plan for what you are going to do. The next three chapters present some approaches for how to do it and how to measure it.

PART 2
Execution

"Great strategy with mediocre execution is mediocre strategy."

CHAPTER 7

Integrated Marketing Is Marketing... and Vice Versa

2013

In corporate America, it's not often you find someone climbing through the ranks into a senior marketing leadership position by starting their career in marketing research. Usually, the path is through sales, finance, or operations. But it has been done, and I wanted to do it.

The Head of Insights at Frito Lay & PepsiCo became the Chief Marketing Officer at Pizza Hut. Years later, the Global Head of Insights at PepsiCo went on to a senior innovation role that spanned across the divisions. These people knew insights, they understood the consumer and the data, and they knew how to apply it all to marketing and innovation.

I had just been promoted to SVP; I had a brand new shiny big title, and I had just assumed responsibility for the essential marketing functions of Strategy, Insights, Creative Services, Brand Planning, Agency Management, and Integrated and Digital Marketing.

But, like in many organizations of this size, these functions operated in silos. Strategy & Insights supported their respective team partners in Marketing, Innovation, and Sales. Creative Services supported their internal partners. Integrated and Digital Marketing, while being supported, were also supporting the same partners, and all still worked separately. So Integrated Marketing wasn't so... integrated.

I had remained committed to the customer for decades and championed customer-first innovation and marketing. So, I wanted to bring this orientation to the new role.

This meant applying our deep understanding of what the customer thought about our brands, whom they trusted, their interests, and where they spent their time learning about our products, to marketing.

Having done a comprehensive customer segmentation study with needs, attitudes, and behaviors, we were able to look at where customers spent their time and craft marketing calendars and content tailored to their interests. Because we knew all of this, we were able to integrate our media buying data to tailor our spending to be as effective as possible.

Yet this was not enough. Our budgets and resources were out of balance. We were spending more time and money on couponing and circulars rather than on digital. Our customers didn't really spend their lives there. So, we shifted resources, engaged with VaynerMedia for community management, published customer-focused content, and a supporting website.

Our marketing effectiveness increased. We achieved a higher return on investment, and we were able to eliminate millions of dollars in wasted spending to re-focus on messaging tailored for the customer.

Our understanding of the customer, and the integration of our insights with our marketing efforts were best in class. We considered it a competitive advantage, and at least for CPG, ahead of its time.

1. Integrated Marketing

Marketing is how we talk about products and brands to our customers. Marketing is how we grow the brand.

Integrated marketing tells your brand story wherever your customers are and when they are ready to hear it—surrounding your customers and prospects with your message.

And we know from survey research that customers value this type of approach. According to a 2018 Zoominfo study[27], more than seven in ten customers say they would prefer to connect with brands through multichannel marketing. Nine out of ten expect consistent interaction across channels.

CPG has always understood the importance of integrated marketing. Integrated marketing surrounds the customer with TV commercials, radio, print coupons, and in-store displays. In the last five years, consumer products companies have upped their game by embracing digital, building content publishing and community management muscle. According to e-Marketer, since 2016, CPG firms have more than doubled their spending on digital advertising.[28]

Tech businesses are evolving as well. For at least the first ten years of its existence, Google never advertised. In fact, it boasted about the fact that it had eclipsed Bing, Yahoo, and other search engines in terms of market share without ever having to spend money on advertising. Back then, if you were a young entrepreneur looking to raise capital for a new start-up, the VCs would often remark words to the effect that "advertising is a waste of money... focus all your money on the product!"

And for many years, start-ups like Netflix, eBay, Amazon, and others took that to heart. But, as the customer media landscape became increasingly fragmented, including more niche media outlets, maturing tech companies realized they had to find new ways to break through the clutter to reach their target customers.

So today, many of the more prominent tech brands are now major customer-facing media brands. Glassdoor, Workday, and Indeed all advertise on TV during large media events, in the way KPMG would show up at the Masters Golf Tournament. SoFi, the personal finance company, started advertising with powerful emotional messages like a classic consumer-facing big brand. Their advertising tugged at the heartstrings with messaging about how SoFi loans can change millennial lives by saving them money on their student loans.

As the media landscape has changed, advertising has also become less expensive. Now, even start-ups realize they have to advertise: mvmt.com, a watch company, advertises on The NHL Network; and MTailor, which can deliver custom-tailored clothing via an app, advertises on The Golf Channel. Dollar Shave Club hammered its target audience with radio advertising, TV, and digital.

2. The Times, They Are A-Changin' – Dramatically

Billions of people make decisions using mobile tools. Most millennials and Gen-Zers are reachable virtually any time on any number of devices. Customers are cord-cutting, and cable (and satellite) companies are now competing with customized commercial-free content from streaming services. A person living in a city thirty years ago saw up to two thousand ad messages a day, compared with up to five thousand today. That's across all channels—print, billboard, radio, TV, etc.[29] There are hundreds of millions of pieces of new content posted to the internet every minute.

Integrated marketing represents the synergy of marketing tactics delivering your brand story and identity across multiple touchpoints.

The marketing tools and tactics available to a marketer now are mind-numbing.

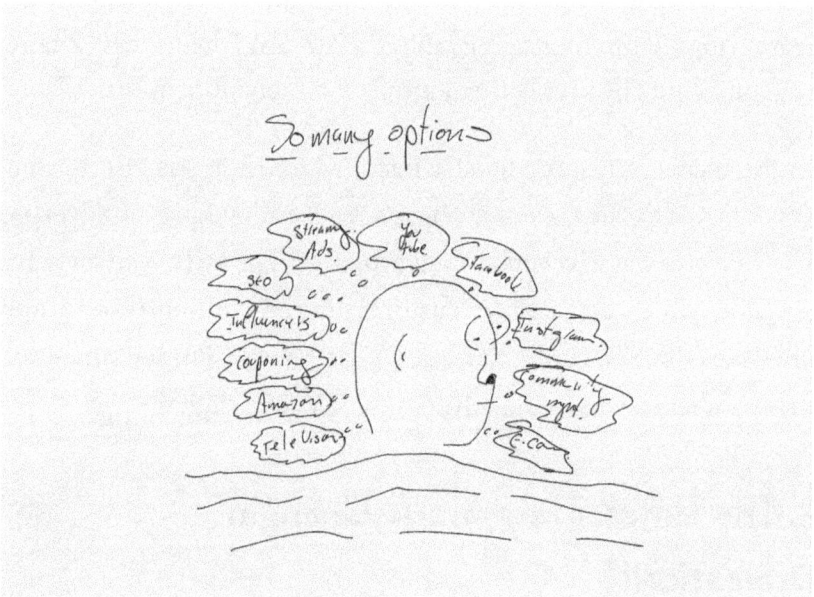

3. The Buyer Journey

The key to integrated marketing is understanding the buyer journey. It seems obvious, but knowing how customers are evaluating buying decisions, and the factors, influences, and preferred sources for that information, is instrumental in getting the message out.

Your content allows your customers to get to know you and relate to your identity. Blogs, videos, whitepapers, ebooks, case studies, and much more tell that story. The content must align to the buyer journey and the entire customer experience.

Sometimes people think the buyer journey and the marketing funnel are different constructs. In fact, they are one and the same. Visually, they may be different, but in practice, they are the same.

There is one crucial difference—the marketing funnel visual suggests that the relationship terminates at the end of Advocacy.

The (Generalized) Marketing Funnel

Awareness

Consideration

Purchase

Experience

Loyalty

Advocacy

I believe in a more recursive shape that is more representative of the influence that comes from advocacy. Aside from awareness, the influence of advocacy may be the most important aspect of integrated marketing.

A loyal customer is more likely to become your next brand advocate if they love your product. And with greater advocacy comes greater brand awareness among new prospects.

Also, what I like about this visual is that it does not imply a destination. Instead, the recursive nature of this buyer journey model reflects the nonlinear nature of marketing. It presents a more dynamic, repeatable process for understanding purchases that leads to loyalty. That process evolves, just as any journey would.

And the loop will continue to repeat itself as long as you are building loyalty by delivering on your brand promise.

The Buyer Journey

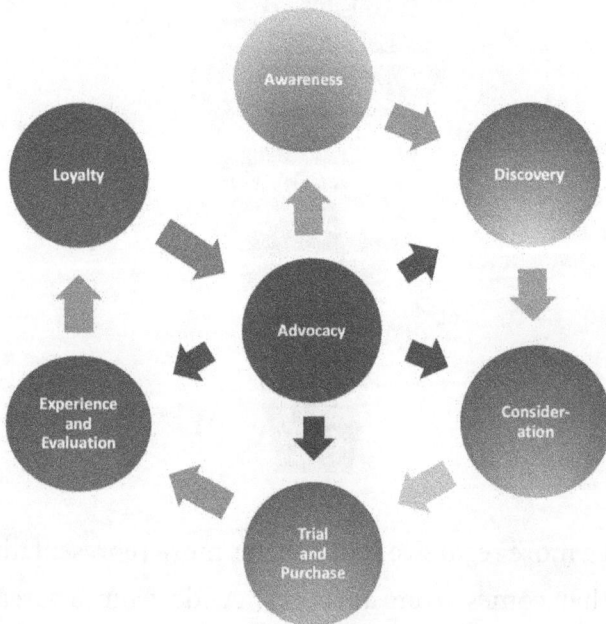

The buyer journey works in B2B purchases decisions as well. The process takes longer and has more people involved in the decision—

especially as the price tag goes up—but it's still the same. And for most products, the higher the price tag, the more advocacy becomes a critical driver.

The buyer journey is the foundation for how integrated marketing tactics and channels work together. As such, they all need to be in place to support the buyer throughout the entire process—from trial to advocacy.

Think of the Buyer Journey in three big phases:

1. Awareness, Discovery, and Consideration
2. Trial, Purchase, Experience, and Evaluation
3. Loyalty and Advocacy

Awareness, Discovery, and Consideration

Nobody will buy your product if they don't know about it. Countless studies have confirmed that top-of-mind awareness is the number-one driver of purchase.

<u>Awareness – Consideration</u>

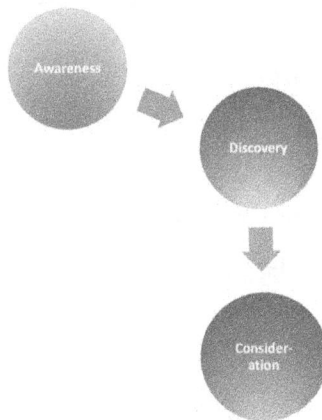

Those brands that create awareness, tell their story, and promote discovery are the ones that work their way into top-of-mind consideration. Each tactic will play potentially different roles throughout the buyer journey. The marketing tactics, in this first phase, need to draw customers in and engage them in order to trigger consideration and purchase.

Building top-of-mind awareness requires an understanding of how the buyer first comes to discover your product. Depending upon the risk, buyers are persistent when it comes to searching out information on a product in which they are interested.

They spend time seeking out information online at your website, and your competitors' websites. Buyers will look at stores and search catalogs, and read the reviews and opinions of influencers and celebrities. In fact, they will "show-room"—by going into stores, exploring, learning, and experiencing the product, then buying it online.

Once you know where the buyer is going for information, you can place your message there. And so, the insights you gain from your market research need to shed light on answering:

- Where is the target customer finding information?
- Who and what sources do the customer trust, and how diligent are they?
- How are the buyers researching their problem? Are they talking to friends, going online, something else?
- Where do they get their news?
- What else do they read off-line?
- What social media do they use, and how often do they use it?

The important thing is that brands need to show up in the marketing channels that customers trust and feel safe using. Customers trying to make a purchase decision tend to trust people like themselves (e.g., birds of a feather.) This kind of advocacy matters because it is more efficient for you and authentic in the eyes of the buyer.

Using eCRM is great. When communicating with your buyers, it is crucial to not just talk "at" your buyers, but to give them a chance to engage. Online chats are great for that purpose. Chatbots are less engaging and potentially damaging to the process if the buyer can't get the information they wanted.

Product reviews are powerful. Getting existing customers to show up in social media on your behalf works. In the last chapter, I mentioned the power of influencers and celebrity endorsements. Social media and Influencer marketing programs (such as those on Instagram) make great use of the stories feature. Snapchat and Instagram's stories allow users to capture and post related images, text, emoticons, and video content.

In November of 2019, *The New York Times* reported that 4.5 million mom influencers were using social media in the United States and that millennial mothers were 18 percent more likely than those from Generation X to rely on advice from their fellow moms.[30]

Long-form content can be successful in avoiding the perception of being another advertisement. Long-form content includes television, storytelling, placing an ad, or promotional content embedded in streaming vehicles, such as Hulu or YouTube. During the Covid-19 crisis, a good number of brands are telling the stories of essential workers and those on the front-lines.

Crowdsourcing video production is a great way to create content to drive awareness. Companies like Mo-film and Tongal engage with large communities of creatives who will create digital content on spec from the brief you create. It's a little more involved than that, but worth the investigation if you are working on a tight budget.

Over a decade ago, BMW was one of the first to successfully create and deploy long-form content with mini-action movies (of their creation) showing their cars in action. Audi has used films from Candide Thovex, a daredevil skier, in an amazing series of YouTube films.

Trial, Purchase, & Experience

Trial and Purchase

Regardless of where the decision is made (direct purchase, through a salesperson, or in-store), the purchase process should be seamless and continue to be supportive of the brand's mission.

Awareness – Experience

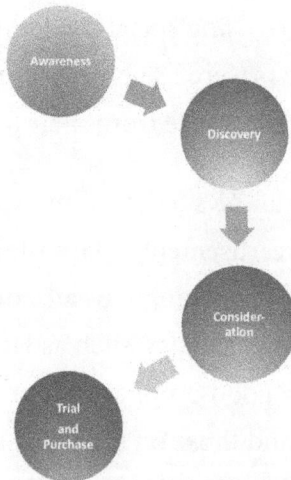

In this phase, research needs to shed light on the content required for buyers to make a purchase decision. Whether the buyer shops retail or buys online, it is essential to understand the:

- Emotional features and benefits sought
- Competitors and their offerings being evaluated
- Market pricing structure

If the buyer is doing their research online or purchasing online, excellent tools like answerthepublic.com offer insight into the natural language that searchers are using to find your site.

For e-commerce, it's about reducing the cart abandonment rate and making sure the customer doesn't leave the page to look at competing prices or more information.

Minimally, using web analytics tools like Google Analytics will reveal:

- How visitors move through the site
- Where visitors bounce out
- How much time visitors spend on a page—indicating engagement and relevance with the content
- What kinds of visitors the brand and site are attracting and what words they are using to find the site

A client of mine had a difficult time with the e-commerce portion of its site. Using basic analytics, we were able to identify the weakest pages using bounce rates, flow, and time spent per page.

Simple adjustments to the drop-down menus improved the flow. Eliminating pages and focusing on content improved the bounce rates. Adjusting the content on key pages improved the time spent per page, and ultimately improved the e-commerce business.

Sites like SEMrush will give you information on the kinds of backlinks that are working and how they need to be improved.

Houzz does a great job of creating a shoppable experience that helps whittle down the multitude of options in the choice set—and it's clickable to make purchases.

In the two images that follow, you'll first see a screenshot with items that are clickable from which you can order. The next image shows the choices and the prices of the item details at the bottom of the screen.

$136.00

$136.00

$886.00

Promise

How marketers deliver on the brand promise varies by industry. In software, customers can be mostly forgiving, when companies opt for a minimum viable product strategy that releases marginally "buggy" products early.

Because tech buyers like to give feedback on new products, bringing a product to market as quickly as possible with the intention to iterate on the fly to improve on the experience is welcomed. Those buyers feel like they are part of the process, and seeing changes that they asked for is part of the reward.

At REI Co-op, the relationship between the associate with the green vest and the buyer is trusting and intimate. For some of my older readers, you might remember the TV jingle that re-enforced the promise, "You can trust your car to the man who wears the star, the big bright Texaco star!"

Similarly, at REI, the implied level of trust conferred onto the associate by the brand, the green vest, is substantial. Customers implicitly trust the sales associates to provide all of the information necessary to make the best equipment purchase.

Let's say you are in the market for a new tent. As you shop around, you are taking stock of two benefits: functional and emotional. The functional benefits are apparent—how much it weighs, whether it can withstand wind gusts, size, etc. For some, the emotional benefit sought might be as simple as the ease of taking a tent out of a car and setting it up quickly. For the hardcore backpacker, there is real satisfaction in finding the right gear (and telling people about it.)

When buyers walk into an REI, they've bought into the promise that REI will outfit them in the best way, because REI knows how.

Loyalty and Advocacy

Repeat buyers become loyal buyers, and loyal buyers hopefully become advocates for the brand. Advocates influence everyone going through the awareness and decision-making process.

According to AC Nielsen, more than 8 in 10 customers around the world say they trust word-of-mouth recommendations from friends and family. That's why authentic reviews on websites are so critical.

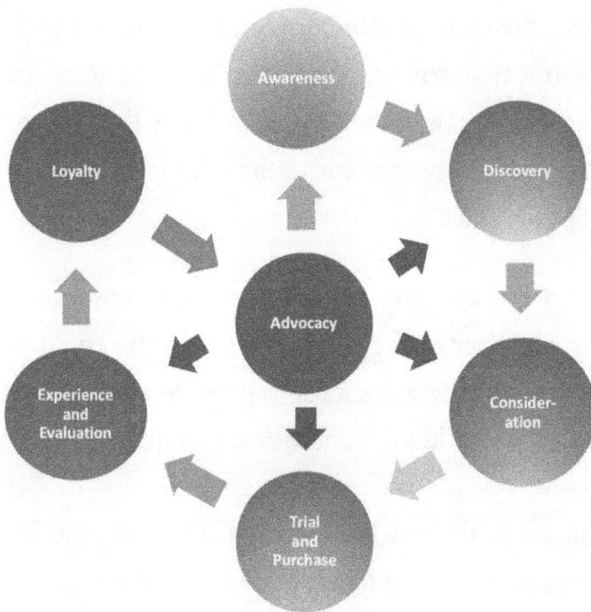

Experience

I am a big believer in intimacy at the moment of trial. For some products that have a higher emotional investment, that risk translates to a heightened level of importance when trying the product for the first time. How the experience feels at that moment is so vital to re-enforcing the promise.

I always felt that the most intimate experience is when a buyer brings a bottled beverage to their lips. It is one of those categories where there is intimacy, as the customer kisses the product at the point of trial—they experience how the shape of the product feels, how it looks, its aroma, its sound, and its touch against their lips.

Every time an end-user downloads a new app for their phone, in those first moments of use, there is hope and expectation that the app will deliver on its promise. Software developers know that the best apps are not always the ones that are the most complex, but the ones that invite users in a more seamless way to experience the full product. The more engaged the user is, the better the experience.

The same is true for just about every category. The experience has to connect the user to the emotional benefits sought when they first bought the product. I can't overemphasize the importance of the moment.

Ever try personal finance software? The promise is immense— control over finances and personal budgets, tracking money spent, ability to see all your accounts in one place, and the opportunity to save money. I've been a long-time user of personal finance software. I started out using Managing Your Money. Then years later, I ported my accounts over to Quicken. Then I moved on to Mint. In each case, the promise was the same. And, in each case, the painful process of importing accounts and assigning spending to categories was personal torture. There were more unfulfilled promises than I can count. I stopped using each product, left the category altogether, and did not provide a ringing endorsement either.

While this experience is a personal one, it is an illustration of a promise unfulfilled and one that has a long-lasting effect on brand and category perception.

Go back to the backpacker who just bought the tent at REI. The backpacker was excited about it, invested in it, went to REI to research it, bought it, and told their friends about it. Then that backpacker went camping, and it rained. The tent did not set up quickly, and the inside got wet. The sleeping bag got wet. It soaked up a lot of water and was cumbersome to carry the next day. Incredibly dissatisfied with his purchase, the backpacker returned the pack to REI used (they have a generous return policy for members) and then told his friends why not to buy it. It was just one experience, but it under-delivered on the promise.

Emotional drivers identified by research need to be fulfilled early on in the experience. That experience re-enforces the brand promise and drives loyalty and advocacy.

Evaluation

Experience codifies the evaluation in the mind of the purchaser. For instance, by now, having read this far in my book, you will be able to decide if it is delivering on its promise. All along, subconsciously, you've been evaluating whether this book is worthy of your time, and whether or not you will tell others about it.

Going back to the backpacker and the tent—our friend, the tent buyer, has now returned the tent. Coincidentally, he also bought a backpack on that trip to REI and loved it. It was lightweight, carried all the necessary gear with room to spare, stayed dry when it rained, and was comfortable. The pack delivered. Now our backpacker friend comes back from his trip in the rain. The first thing he does is goes on REI.com and writes a review. He gives the pack five stars and the tent one star. Then he goes on YouTube and does a video review of his gear that he just tried out.

Those two reviews will influence many future pack and tent buyers. And our backpacker will feel good because he told everyone about his experience.

Most brands in the recreational industry have taken to adding pro voices to their product descriptions. Pro voices are verified experts in an industry vertical who talk about particular products' (e.g., trail running shoes) performance, durability, and overall rating.

This is why Amazon's reviews are so critical in the purchasing process. Positive reviews bolster potential buyers' confidence in the choices they are making, mitigating buyer's remorse and returns. Negative reviews keep buyers from making mistakes.

Bazaarvoice's tools encourage customers to share their opinions and experiences about your products, wherever they shop, and thus enable you to reach more people and influence more purchases. Your advocates will be the most trusted source of information for people who are considering the purchase. It establishes your brand as non-invasive, transparent, and trustworthy.

When others talk about your brand and post links back to your websites, it improves your credibility, and more importantly the likelihood of purchase.

Advocacy feeds upon itself because it is shared not just once but many times. In forwarded links, positive reviews will help brands find new customers.

Two-Way Dialogue

Reviews are crucial, but they are pretty much a one-way dialogue. While brands can respond with thanks or attempt to soften negative reviews, they really need to keep a two-way conversation going. Brands need a variety of forums in which to interact with customers.

Most brands start that dialogue on Facebook or Instagram. I feel the best place to start is at home with your proprietary assets—your website. Here is where you can control almost everything— especially the content you post. You can refresh that content as needed and invite patrons to participate in the dialogue, not only with each other but with the brand as well. Having that dialogue on your own website helps to bolster brand affinity without ever having to do endless web searches. Pure e-commerce companies must use their proprietary assets to keep an open line of communication with the customer to maintain a long-lasting brand relationship. Pure e-com businesses also control the flow of movement on their website. Smart analytics can drive conversion throughout the buyer journey.

Marketing Automation

As prospective buyers and existing customers come to your website, collect data. Collect as much as you can to learn about what they are seeking. Then, customize your message on your website, and improve your targeting or product to meet their needs. As I said earlier, chatbots have become increasingly more prevalent, as they collect data and the interests of the customers doing their searches.

That data, in turn, improves the accuracy and actionability of your content.

There is an inherent value (and expense) in applying marketing automation and customer relationship management to the many routine aspects of the buyer journey. And these costs are decreasing as companies figure out how better to target and engage customers on the fly. Check out HubSpot and Marketo to learn a more about marketing automation.

Content

Above all else, what makes content great is that it adds value to the reader. Does it make the readers smarter? Help them solve a problem? Make them laugh or provide entertainment value? Adding value also means that what you are saying is original, authentic, and transparent by being anchored in the truth.

Content should re-enforce your brand positioning. It helps connect the brand, at least perceptually, if not in reality, to what really matters.

The holy grail is that if your content is good, others will create new content from it. Not only will they re-post it, but they will also build upon it. The backlinks others place in their newsletters, or articles, or even in their own social creates new content continues to build upon and spread your message without you spending an incremental dime. It also improves your findability.

There are firms who specialize in developing content. Agencies like Vaynermedia are full service, but there are others where you can do a lot of learning on your own or get different levels of help from them. While I've never used their paid services, I'm a big fan of the level of learning you can get from Contently.

Social Media

While social media is perfect for fostering that dialogue, not every social media channel should be treated the same. It is essential to know which social channels will best help you reach your target. Here is a very brief overview, but you can find a lot more depth elsewhere.

Facebook helps you develop and foster a sense of community between you and your customers. It helps you build loyalty and advocacy. Having your fans talk to each other is the best way to influence others.

Twitter is a casual way for you and others to talk about your brand. Twitter can help you understand pain points and provide conversation on the brand. Increase the frequency of your tweets, and encourage others to do the same.

Instagram helps build brands through visual expression and community. The platform has exploded in recent years with brands as Facebook starts to feel a little "older" and restrictive in the way it allows brands to reach users. Instagram encourages customers to participate more expressively than Twitter and reaches a more mature audience than Snapchat or TikTok.

YouTube is a valuable place to share your longer-form content. Use it for broadcasting information, product demonstrations, and short films.

Pinterest is more of a visual search platform and community platform. It has a heavily female and mom-focused userbase. People who come to Pinterest do so to help make decisions in a purchase. As such, users are open to new brands, new products, and inspiration for new ideas.

Snapchat and TikTok are geared toward Gen-Z, are more playful tools, and blur the lines of their competitors that have been around longer. While both are heavily video driven, TikTok is primarily for short, fifteen-second videos, whereas Snapchat is more robust and focused on bundling messaging, photo-sharing, social media, search, entertainment, news, location services, and more. Snap has new partnerships with the NBA, the NFL, and NBCUniversal to create original programming, and has a mapping feature with millions of local business listings.

All these major social media channels will help get the word out and build advocacy. By matching the social media channel, brands are reaching new audiences, finding less competition, and connecting with influencers to drive new relationships. Once fledgling social media sites, these channels now have billions of installs and millions of views daily.

The power of these sites goes beyond the users. Data-mine these sites for insight to learn more about your customers for better targeting and improved messaging.

4. The Marketing Calendar and Stacking Tactics

Social media channels are just one of many tactics that are part of integrated marketing. At a high level, each of the steps in the buyer journey will require using a few tactics to surround and reach the customer.

Tactics are like bricks. You can't build a building with just one. They have to be stacked on top of another.

The same is true in the buyer decision-making process. Stacking tactics means making sure you are surrounding customers with a compelling message in the many areas they are likely to see it. Each tactic re-enforces the next one, and the synergy of the tactics has a more considerable influence on the buying decision than any individual tactic alone.

But if the message isn't consistent, and the tactics don't show up where the customer is, and if it isn't connected to the other tactics, the synergy between the tactics will not be there.

A consistent message needs to be salient. Salience is more than just relevance. Salience is the brand's connection to the customer's pain point or needs. That means the message you've selected for your integrated marketing is a carefully constructed link between the brand identity and customer needs.

Be mindful that your tactics must be objective-driven. An easy way to make sure of that is to align your KPIs with your marketing tactics. Are you driving awareness? Equity? Sales? Loyalty? When you build your program, build it with your objectives in mind.

The Marketing Brief

One of the best ways to make sure your message is consistent is with a marketing brief. Marketing briefs are internal documents shared with agencies or the internal team that describe the situation, the objective, and goals. While the brief needs focus, it also needs to allow the creative team the latitude to create without being boxed into a single idea or expression.

A great brief may include:

- Business situation
- Assignment
- Marketing objectives
  - Goals
  - Metrics
- Target audience
- Core insight
- The competitive frame of reference
- Key customer benefit
- Brand personality and tone
- Brand positioning

Objectives should be measurable and achievable. I can recall a time when all of our goals were outrageously aggressive and unachievable, and thus set the year up for failure. So, make sure the targets are within reach—or else risk missing them and demoralizing all those who worked on the effort.

If you're driving brand identity, it's best to pick the channels that give you the most visual impact and the ones that allow you to tell a story.

The Marketing Calendar

Now that we have gone through the buyer journey, we know what we want to say, to whom we want to say it, and where we want to say it. We've done some pretty good work.

The next step is focused on timing, the number, and frequency of exposures on video and radio, the logistics of pulsing those exposures, and supporting those with tactical digital. The channel tactics you select must work with each other to amplify the message you are driving.

Here is a hypothetical calendar that illustrates how a big brand might pulse media and support with other tactics.

Tactics	Jan	Feb	Mar	Apr	May	Jun	Jul	Aug	Sep	Oct	Nov	Dec
Weeks	4	8	12	16	20	24	28	32	36	40	44	52
National TV												
On-Line Video												
Paid Search												
eCRM												
Market Automation												
Public Relations												
Social												
Facebook												
Radio												
Satellite												
Broad Cast												

That said, your data should point to how and when to pulse media. Are you a seasonal brand, a holiday brand, one that gets the greatest exposure in the evening when customers are browsing or streaming? Use these kinds of data to build your calendar.

5. Sounding Like a Broken Record Yet?

Go back to the quote by Drucker: "The aim of marketing is to <u>know and understand the customer so well</u> the product or service fits them and sells itself."

Every tactic and every ad placement is informed by data analytics and insights. With a great understanding of the customer—how they make decisions, what problems they're trying to solve, and where they get their information—tactics deployed along the buyer journey will be informed and effective, and drive advocacy.

"Packaging can be theater; it can create a story."

—Steve Jobs

CHAPTER 8

WYSIWYG

(What You See Is What You Get)

1986

In the movie, *The Graduate*, Dustin Hoffman plays a character by the name of Benjamin Braddock, a recent college graduate. In one scene, Benjamin is at a graduation party at his parents' house when a family friend, Mr. McGuire, pulls him aside and says, "I have just one word for you. Plastics!" Mr. McGuire was encouraging Benjamin to have a career in plastics.

Years later, echoing Mr. McGuire, my grandfather, at his fiftieth-anniversary party, essentially said to me, "I got one word for you. Merchandising!"

Merchandising!

My grandfather was all about merchandising. When I was younger, we would drive together in his old Cadillac Seville from Philadelphia down I-295 to our butcher shop in Delaware. It's a pretty long ride, and he would regale me with times of old and instruct me on how to be successful when it was my time to run the business. He would talk endlessly about merchandising—how the product was merchandised, how the product was placed, what it was placed next to, how it helped his customers make decisions, and how all of that helped us sell.

Packaging Is Merchandising

Packaging sells. It communicates and supports brand imagery. It transfers its expression to the product inside, and back to the brand.

1. A Box Is Not a Box – A Bottle Is Not Just a Bottle

Packaging, when done right, is powerful.

- Physical packaging can promote changes in behavior by making it easier to access, transport, or use.
- The visuals and words on packaging tell your story, support your positioning, and reinforce the attitudes and beliefs about your product.
- When properly integrated into the customer buyer journey, it promotes awareness, trial, and a positive user experience.
- Optimizing the packaging process can help improve margins and profits.

In 1951, scientific researcher and clinical psychologist Louis Cheskin wrote the groundbreaking book *Color for Profit,*[31] which was one of the first to recognize a scientific approach to color and design.

Cheskin wrote about the concept of *sensation transference,* which describes the individual impact of each element of a package. For instance, blue means cool or cold and transfers the coolness to the brand's imagery and product. A calligraphy font type transfers elegance to that brand.

In 2018, the Paper and Packaging Board and IPSOS commissioned a survey and found that 7 in 10 (72 percent) of customers agree that packaging design can influence their purchasing decision.[32] Great packaging has the ability to line up with the physical or lifestyle needs of customers. When Starbucks decided to eliminate plastic straws, it needed a way to offer the functionality of a straw to those with physical handicaps. So, they created a new form of packaging: a coffee cup with a built-in sip lid.

2. Packaging and Brand Identity

Packaging helps tell the brand story and create a deeper, more personal bond between the brand and the customer. Buyers like to know more about their brands, what's in them, how they're made, and their origin. And, they're looking for those visual cues that support the brand's RTBs.

Regardless of the product category or where it is sold, the package represents the brand. The font, the color, the material, the size, and every single word should be thoughtfully chosen.

In consumer goods, the front of the package represents all of the imagery associated with the brand. The back and sides of the package help to tell the brand story and help satisfy customer curiosity about ingredients and usage. Sometimes the story is a short vignette about who developed it (e.g., Amy's Kitchen), or maybe it describes the manufacturing process and how the company sources its ingredients. Coors beer is famous for having the Rocky Mountains on its packaging because it uses mountain spring water from the Rocky Mountains in the brewing process.

Let's look at the package for GT'S Pure Love Kombucha. This package does a great job of first communicating the brand and the product. Getting up close, the front of the package expresses all the supportive context for the purchasing and consumption experience.

3. Clutter

Packaging is an important driver, especially when the shelves are crowded with numerous choices. Good packaging sets help customers distinguish between competing alternatives and make shopping easier. Between 1975 and 2008, the number of products in the average supermarket swelled from an average of 8,948 to almost 47,000, according to the Food Marketing Institute, a trade group.[33]

The impact that packaging has on shelving is so important that large CPG companies have transformed warehouses into test stores and use observational market research to watch buyers shop and see how they interact with the packages and shelf sets.

New research methodologies have emerged to simulate the impact shelf sets have on purchase. Eye-tracking research watches the flow of the eye when looking at the package. It determines what the person looks at first and second, and follows the eyes as they examine the package. Neuromarketing research uses caps with electrodes to determine how the brain processes imagery and how it affects buyer perceptions.

In all these methods, predictive modeling is used to determine which attributes/elements have the most impact on purchase. Ultimately, this optimizes the communication impact of the package.

Buyers are making decisions on what they see. In a store, it is difficult to take in a typical broad shelf of items at a glance. Most shoppers are not spending time looking at the full shelf set. They are looking for the familiar or for something that catches their eye.

This is even more true of the decision-making process online, where buyers are making decisions on products looking at small pictures of product packaging. Deciding if something is premium or value? Frivolous or serious?

Let's look at a few examples.

Nearly $900 million is spent on snack bars every year in the United States. From 2011 to 2015, this category saw 2,731 new product introductions.[34]

Snack bars are one of the most crowded product sections in a grocery store. But take a look at what Larabar, Cliff, and Epic have done. By adopting clean packaging principles, they help solve the shelf clutter problem. They also create a brand block—a mini-advertising billboard on the shelf, which makes it easier for customers to find their brand.

For brand loyalists, they're able to find their favorite product with less distraction, and as a result, will be less likely to switch out to other brands.

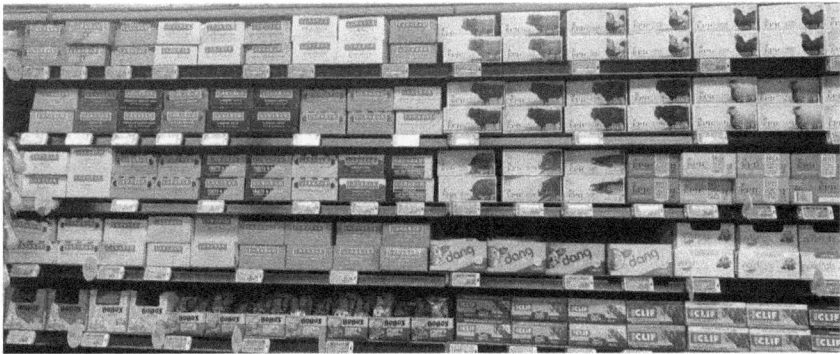

Tea products are another crowded product category in retail stores. Take a look at what Yogi Tea and Traditional Medicinals have done to alleviate the perception of clutter.

They adopt clean lines on their packaging that are consistent and easy on the eyes. Even at this distance, you can see the separation between the different brands of tea.

4. Occasion or Need-Based Shelving

Although not as common as Brand Blocking, you can organize products by specific occasion or need. Occasions include the time of day (e.g., beer for happy hour or coffee every morning) or holidays (e.g., champagne for New Year's).

If you visit your local pharmacy, you may notice that the over-the-counter drug aisle is organized by need (e.g., cold, flu, allergy). Pet stores also tend to be organized this way. You will often find some shelves and product lines arranged by the need or health condition or life stage (e.g., eyes, hips, etc.).

Take a closer look at tea again. Yogi tea is also grouped by the needs that correspond to various health benefits. For example, all the green teas are grouped together because they all have excellent antioxidant properties. Likewise, all the chamomile teas are grouped because they all are excellent sleep aids. So, within seconds, you can figure out exactly what's what and make a selection.

E-commerce is often organized by needs.

REI.com does something similar by organizing products by need, form, and function, such as those for camping, climbing, and cycling.

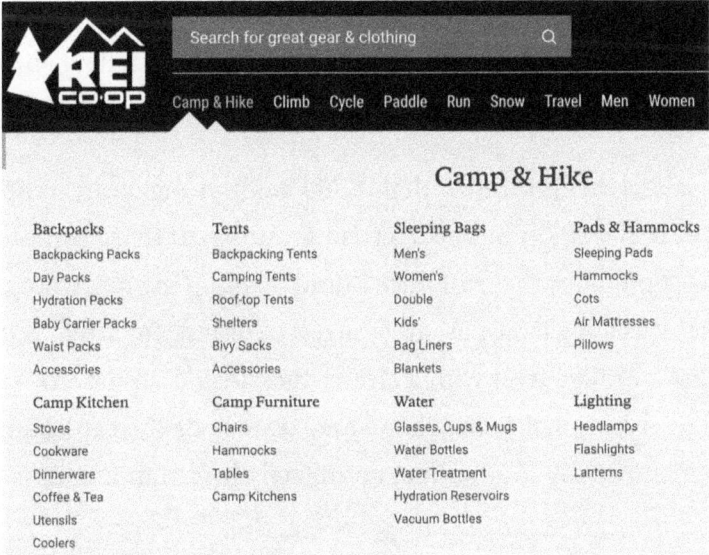

But the world's largest online retailer, Amazon, bucks this trend. Despite all its positive attributes, its store isn't very shoppable. Its show-as-many-products-as-possible strategy is a deliberate attempt to provide incredible depth, breadth, and access—holding shoppers on the site to promote more impulse purchasing.

5. Ch, ch, ch... Changes

Making changes to packaging is a significant undertaking, which is why brands don't make them often. Changing a package design is a costly and time-consuming process. It should not be done just for the sake of change.

For well-established brands with a core clientele, packaging changes can confuse the customer and make the product harder to find, especially when customers are used to looking for the same cues on the package they had been using for decades.

In 2009, PepsiCo's Tropicana brand learned a similar, more painful lesson of package redesign.[35] In early January of 2009, Tropicana decided to launch a new design for its best-selling product, Tropicana Pure Premium.

With sales reaching more than $700 million per year, Tropicana invested $35 million in an advertising campaign that promoted the new packaging for the fruit juice brand. Among the more noticeable changes was a big transparent glass full of orange juice that replaced the classic orange fruit with a straw stuck inside on the front of the package. Additionally, the shape and texture of the cap changed. I can remember my mother just completely lost, standing in front of the orange juice cold case trying to find my father's favorite orange juice. She was used to searching for it by the color of the cap.

But just a few days into the campaign, customers started criticizing the new design, especially on social networks. Sales dropped more than 20 percent, and on February 23, just six weeks into the new design, Tropicana announced that it would return to its original packaging design. In total, this initiative cost Tropicana more than $50 million.

Packaging changes usually are favorable, and the impact of a good packaging change can be meaningful. Ola Brew is a local Hawaiian company with great local brand recognition. Ola Brew launched its Hawaiian Hard Seltzer in Hawaii, where the competition for the brand and its space would not be challenged. However, the company was looking to expand into new territories and would find itself against some significant competition. It needed to refresh its package to break through the clutter, and tell its story.

The recessive colors of Ola's original packaging would not break through the clutter of a crowded shelf. Many of the competitors have similar white backgrounds (which became a category convention when Anheuser-Busch launched its all-silver/white can). Another problem was that Ola's Hawaiian brand identity centered around authentic Hawaiian ingredients, sourced from Hawaiian farmers. The picture of the islands was not clear, and the unique and familiar Hawaiian horizon was missing.

The new design remedies these problems. Color-coded band lines at the top communicate flavor. The multiple bold colors help the brand stand out and communicate Hawaiian authenticity in words and visually.

6. Packaging Materials

The materials of the package can play an important role in supporting brand identity.

PepsiCo did a number of futures studies to look at where packaging trends might take the brand. The study explored different shapes, portion sizes, materials and imagery.

Semiotics experts look at and decode the shapes, symbols, colors, sizes, fonts, and other "signals" to help interpret trends in packaging. One project explored new delivery mechanisms for water and shapes for tea packaging. Gatorade's product innovation not only changes the shape of the product but the package as well.

In 2007, Mountain Dew launched the Green Label Art series, a limited-edition series of aluminum bottles featuring designs created by a variety of artists. It was the first time a carbonated soft drink was packaged in an aluminum bottle in the U.S.

Seventh Generation's mission is to transform the world into a healthy, sustainable, and equitable place for the next seven generations. Their packaging supports that mission with recyclable bottles and easy dose systems to minimize waste.

Apple's iPhone boxes are so elegant because Apple's Industrial Design division often takes a lead role in crafting the packaging that supports the product. In addition, some of the materials are compostable and sustainable, with minimal materials and no extra paper or user manuals.

The Amazon brand's iconic smile is ever-present on all of its packaging and is supportive of its customer satisfaction mission.

Waiting for an Amazon package, for many, is an anticipatory (seemingly daily) event. It's no surprise—there is a smile waiting on every doorstep around the world.

"The price of anything is the amount of life you exchange for it."
—Henry David Thoreau

CHAPTER 9

Pricing

2012

I'm talking to the team about pricing. We've tackled pricing before in a narrower fashion. What we were taking the team through now was the next pricing work, which was completely different. It was massive. It cut across every category and every brand. It touched not just our brands but had to measure the pricing impact and responses of our competitors.

This was not a trade-off analysis or a Van Westendorp technique. This was the modeling of sales and revenue data for each product, every SKU, at every major retailer and in every geography.

To further complicate this, we managed to hire more than one of the largest pricing firms in the United States to do the same thing—a little differently. Alongside this process, our sales and customer marketing team hired its trusted vendor to perform the same analysis using different methods.

The amount of money and people and time dedicated to this effort was substantial. Aside from the corporate dysfunction, why would we go to all this trouble? Because getting pricing right is hard, and *that* important.

Our leading brands had to maintain or increase share profitably. Our middle market brands had to compete and gain share, and our value brands had to find ways to survive.

What else? Pricing had to be clear enough to create a distinction between channels. The leading retailer in the value channel would have the lowest price. Other value retailers would then be priced at a slightly higher price point, and with a slightly different product configuration.

This was incredibly complex and valuable. We made mistakes, we learned and corrected. Sometimes we didn't make corrections in planning and had to make corrections in the market after the fact.

What follows are the concepts, considerations, and thinking we went through developing our pricing strategy.

1. Pricing Discipline

Pricing is a discipline that cascades down from your business strategy and objectives. Managing pricing allows you to optimize your share, margins, and profitability, and re-invest in marketing (and the business).

- When you don't re-invest in marketing, there is a genuine risk that competition will grab a share of mind and wallet.

- When you don't invest in innovation, there is a real risk that customers will start looking for alternatives to your product if not adequately supported by messaging, promotions, and sales initiatives.

- When a category or business is starting to suffer a downturn, companies tend to have a knee-jerk reaction to tighten up on spending. Some adopt a "burn the furniture" strategy of pulling money out of all of the discretionary spending. This can be crippling. When the downturn starts to cycle up, your brand has been out of the customer's mind and marketplace precisely at the time it needed to be there.

- Spending on marketing into downturns is what smart pricing strategy enables.

From a growth marketing perspective, smart pricing allows you to:

- Invest in equity development
- Invest in promoting buyer journey marketing activities – especially awareness and loyalty-building activities
- Invest in product refreshes and new product development

2. The Basics

The basics of finding the right price point are more complex than simply looking at elasticities. But let's start there and then talk a little bit about pricing strategy.

In chart 2-1, four brands are shown. You can see that the category, for the most part, is pretty inelastic (meaning price increases don't affect demand a great deal).

Chart 2-1: Price-Share Curves

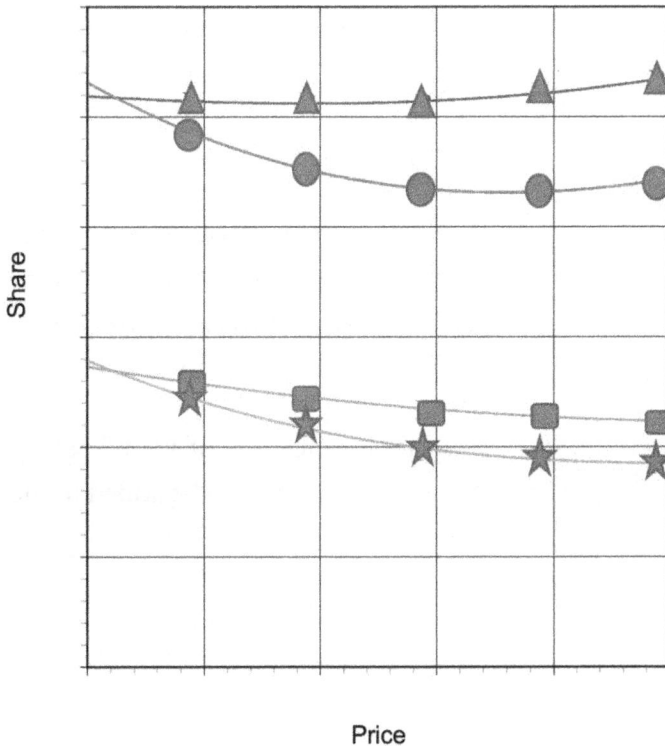

The product represented by the triangle is a dominant brand and holds the largest share of the market. Pricing does not hurt its business. It may even benefit from a pricing halo. That is, the higher price implies a product of higher quality. So, pricing at a higher price point to optimize profit is a good strategy for this brand.

The product represented by the circle is price sensitive, and revenue drops when its price increases. The products represented by the square and star are lesser players in the category. Both, to a lesser extent, are affected by increases in price. For this latter group of brands, optimizing pricing is a little more challenging. Clearly, we would take the necessary steps to model them out further, to find the place where volume and profit are optimized.

Chart 2-2 is a simple display of the volume and profit curves at various price changes. The goal is to maximize profit at an acceptable volume decline that does not risk losing too many customers to competition or damaging brand equity.

Hypothetically, with this brand, the place where there is an acceptable volume decline and significant profit upside represents an opportunity to increase the price. In this case, a price increase of ~7% drops volume 5% but delivers a profit of +9%.

If customers migrate down to another one of your less expensive brands in the portfolio, then that profit would be added to the profit gains here.

Chart 2-2: Price Optimization

Price Optimization
Volume-Profit Trade-off

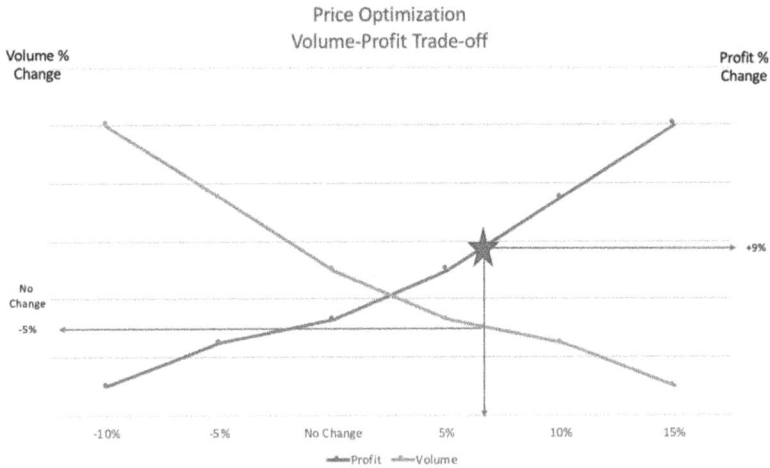

3. Newton's Law of Pricing

No, Issac Newton actually didn't have a law on pricing. But, if he had, it might have said something to the effect that if you are in a highly competitive space, a price increase or decrease will definitely solicit a significant competitive reaction.

If you're not the market leader and you plan to undercut a market leader in an attempt to steal share, expect a reaction from the market leader. The leader has more flexibility in pricing. They can come down in price or promote heavily to make you rethink an aggressive pricing decision.

I've seen this on more than one occasion. When a new brand or product entered the chip market, Frito Lay would squeeze them out at the shelf with all of their pricing power. They could increase promotion spending, deploy more trade money to reduce the available shelf space, or lower their price aggressively.

4. Becoming a Price Leader

A market leader with a strong brand (e.g., share and health), can shape pricing for the entire category. The size of the brand alone creates a wake for others to follow, either up or down. So, if the leader makes a price increase, others can and will follow its moves.

Brands with strong equity and low elasticity, like the triangle brand in chart 8-1, have the power to choose to be a price leader—that is, to set the category's pricing structure.

However, a strong brand with high elasticity should be patient and treat pricing carefully, wary not to damage existing brand equity by overestimating pricing power. Don't overreach. Be disciplined and improve margins to generate cash to invest back into the business. It will also be reasonably easy to follow the leader if the price leader makes a move. Just be mindful of the price gaps between the two brands. Too close and your customers might jump ship and migrate to the price leader (for implied quality or brand equity.) Too far away and you'll be leaving money on the table. These brands would reside in the upper left quadrant.

Now, if you have a brand with low price elasticity, but the brand has the potential to play a more prominent role in the buyer's mind, then there is a future for pricing improvement down the road. This may be either because it is unique, because it has a sustainable/appealing mission, or for some other reason that promises long term growth—no need to be aggressive. Play follow the leader and maintain price gaps close enough to nibble at the heels of the leader—and steal share slowly.

A high-elasticity/low-equity brand is of questionable value. These brands typically have low margins and are playing a different role in the portfolio, such as covering broad costs of manufacturing or labor. A value brand with good equity, but with a customer base that does not have deep pockets to pay more, will have trouble increasing the price.

If the industry is crowded with many competitors, you may choose to differentiate yourself by being a price leader or following the coattails of price leaders. Or you may be locked into a price war. Price wars are very common in the highly competitive telecom industry. Switching occurs regularly as customers seek the lowest cost and highest benefit deals. So, pricing may need to consider which competitive brands are most vulnerable to switching.

To be a price leader, it helps to:

- Have the product features and benefits to support the price point
- Have a solid share position in your category. While dominance is not critical, it can be challenging to sustain price leadership without volume.
- Have or be in a category where the price elasticity is low so that high price points or increases will not result in dramatic volume or share losses. In commodity businesses, this can be challenging where every few cents can lead to brand switching.
- Be in a category that is stable or growing.

Being a price leader also means you are implying that you are not only offering the right features and benefits for your target audience but also that the product will be of high quality.

In the food and beverage industry, this means quality ingredients. In the technology industry, it means not being buggy. In apparel, it means the stitching stays stitched.

5. Gap Pricing

Not the clothing store. I have to say, when it came to managing price gaps to competition, the sales and customer marketing teams at Del Monte, and later at Big Heart Pet Brands, were the best I have ever seen.

What they were able to do was find the price gaps within our portfolio necessary to optimize profitability *within* it, and maximize the volume potential by finding the right spacing between *competitive* brands in the market. They were not always perfect, but they were pretty solid for sure.

It seems obvious, but managing the gaps within your product portfolio allows you to manage migration and minimize cannibalization. Pricing too close to one another risks cannibalization from less profitable products and heightens the risk that the customers of your more valuable products might migrate out.

If one product in your portfolio has higher margins than your other brands, ensure that you are driving customers to the most profitable one. One way to do this is by pricing the value brand a little higher and offering fewer benefits—just enough to keep the most valuable customers buying the more expensive products.

You see this strategy with service-as-a-subscription products. The approach is pretty simple. The first level has few features and is free. The next one up costs a bit more, but more is offered. Then if the customer needs, even more, they'll upgrade and pay more for the added features.

If the buyers make comparisons with competitive products, they will find similar structures. Buyers then have to make their decisions on the brand strength and features of the product offering.

6. Trial and Adoption Pricing

Pricing models to support new products and drive adoption have their own set of unique challenges compared to existing products.

Most early adoption models launch with value pricing to gain users quickly and to establish a foothold in the marketplace. Many start-ups take this strategy with their minimum viable product (MVP) so that they can build a user base quickly.

New-product pricing might adopt a "wait and see" approach by launching the product, using initial customer feedback to figure out the optimal price. Then, they'll course correct quickly as needed, eventually through trial and error arriving at an optimal price point that maximizes profit/revenue or volume.

7. Growth First — Price Later Corollary

If you are a start-up venture, you may choose to adopt a growth-first strategy that ignores pricing (and profits) to gain market share. It took Facebook five years and over $800 million in venture capital money before it was profitable.[36]

Start-ups that adopt a growth-first strategy also tend to take a minimum viable product approach that emphasizes continuous product releases to validate hypotheses on product design, functionality, customer discovery, and acceptance. As products continue to be refined, pricing evolves as well.

8. Pricing Impact on Managing Supply and Demand

Complex financial pricing models are often built to gauge the impact of increasing and decreasing prices on supply and demand. Lowering prices stimulate demand, but increased demand may create shortages if your supply chain is not capable of handling such demand.

Ridesharing services, for instance, need to manage their demand and supply tightly. In the past, they have found themselves unable to meet demand because they didn't have enough drivers. To some extent, surge pricing mitigates that problem. It increases prices to suppress demand. That way, they can match the number of drivers available to the customers willing to pay the surge pricing.

9. Channel Pricing

Products sold directly to the customer can be priced lower because they eliminate the retailer. There are other substantial fulfillment costs, but typically there is more flexibility with e-commerce.

But those lower online prices still are subject to the threat of comparison shopping. Comparison shopping occurs when the buyers become uncertain that they are getting the best price; it is the number-one reason why online shoppers abandon their cart. So, it is essential to do the necessary work to see where your products fit relative to the competition.

Products sold through an intermediary, such as food & grocery and traditional retail, have other challenges impacted by things such as trade costs and physical space constraints. Trade cost is the cost of doing business and includes the cost of promotions and shelf discounts. The more you spend, the better your visibility and placement are on shelves, end caps, and special displays.

Channel pricing also extends to the concept of product-market fit. Where the product can be purchased and where it competes have a lot to do with how it is priced.

Traditional grocery stores typically operate on thin profit margins. This explains why you don't find luxury goods at Walmart. Thus, the channel has a significant impact on the products you sell and the price you charge. If your competition is Walmart, you need to be mindful of its lowest cost leader strategy. Additionally, if your competition is Amazon, you have to understand how its "long tail" inventory strategy impacts pricing decisions.

10. The Long Tail of E-commerce

For companies that have broad product portfolios, one of the most critical and difficult decisions they make is whether to keep, replace, or retire products on a physical shelf because of low sales.

Traditional retailers make most of their money selling just a few of the products that have faster turns and make up the most volume. Products where brands spend more money and don't get the turns end up spending money on trade discounts.

E-commerce effectively eliminated that challenge. Since there are no trade or shelving costs and shelf space is limitless, there is no risk to your higher turning products. As long as it makes sense to make the product, you can make it available to sell online.

This concept was first popularized by Chris Anderson in an October 2004 issue of *Wired* magazine. Anderson elaborated on the concept in his book *The Long Tail: Why the Future of Business Is Selling Less of More*.[37]

11. Reminders Work

I had the good fortune of working on a simple pricing project for a popular beverage. I was asked to design a pricing study for a unique pack size. Nothing complicated.

I ran a quick trade-off exercise using multiple price points, some options for in-pack promotions, and a few more bells and whistles. Pretty straightforward.

The results came back. Don't change the price, just throw in a coupon.

Sometimes, all you have to do is remind customers that you have a product on the shelf and entice them to come back when they run out.

Similarly, with any e-commerce, staying ever present with small promotions keeps you top of mind with customers, without denigrating margins.

12. Pricing Is Marketing

If nothing else, you realize that pricing is more than just optimizing volume and profit. Elasticities are only part of it. Pricing strategy is multidimensional, and care needs to be taken when figuring out how to optimize it. It's not simply a mathematical problem—it's a marketing problem.

"You can't manage what you can't measure."
—Peter Drucker

CHAPTER 10

It Works

1984

I worked for Don Bruzzone right after moving to California. Don was a great person to work for and a wonderful man. He was generous with his time and his knowledge.

Don came out of the agency world and had developed an innovative technique for measuring advertising impact. Called "day after" recall (DAR), he sent out images of advertising in a mail survey (remember those?) to respondents. I developed structural equation models to prove his belief that day after recall was an effective technique for measuring awareness impact of advertising. We later worked with David Aaker, of the Haas business school, to develop the theory behind the model. Mail surveys were falling out of favor even in 1984, so it was getting harder and harder to get the business community to believe in the tool. Don's DAR technique was just one of many that consultants were using to prove the effectiveness of advertising.

Since those days, as an insights leader and consultant, one of my roles has been to prove that advertising and marketing works. It is not uncommon to run into a C-suite or Finance function that is maniacally focused on the return on investment from the marketing.

One of my more recent roles illustrates this struggle beautifully.

I had been brought into my new role by a CMO whose focus was to step-change marketing and be a change agent for the company. We both believed in customer-centric marketing and innovation, and fortunately for me, he believed in marketing research to drive and measure it.

He bet heavily on the actions he was taking to transform the company into a customer-centric marketing organization. His approach to marketing was solid CPG thinking, grounded in insight, with deep marketing learning. There was new branding, new marketing initiatives, and new advertising.

Yet, the "proof is in the pudding." We needed proof that the increase in marketing spending was worthwhile. So, we launched a major effort to measure the impact quarterly.

We researched vendors to help us with the initiative. We interviewed all the well-known companies and a few of the boutique ones as well. Each had their own approach, and all had been validated. They were all running models that had a high level of statistical validity. Models that "fit." So, picking among them was not an easy task.

I, also, hadn't expected to find so many inside the company wanting to be involved with the work. Which was great. I didn't want to mistake enthusiasm for politics, but I knew it was important to find the right partners to help drive the work. Our finance team had really smart people who knew how to use the work when it was done. They were the right partners for the job.

Early on, the models didn't make sense, and I was questioning whether or not we'd selected the right vendor. Kevin Clancy used to say something to the effect, "If it smells like a fish, it probably is one." So, we had to keep going back to the vendor to improve the face validity of the models. Statistical validity alone wasn't cutting it.

Finally, the models improved. They became more predictive. And we were able to get the return on marketing investment with both statistical validity and face validity. Then we were able to adjust tactics and spending to have a greater impact. We got so good at it that we eventually ran the models with more frequency and included more and more marketing levers. Even though the organization and leadership would change, the desire to measure the impact of and improve marketing remained.

1. Burden of Proof

The burden of proving that marketing works is on the shoulders of the marketer. Marketing works in a couple of fundamental ways:

a) The impact it has on volume and revenue
b) The impact on bolstering equity and presence in the market

In addition, the impact with retailers or distributors who want to know that you are spending behind the brand matters—if you're not supporting the product, why would they want to carry it?

For the most part, we focus on the first two. The third is measured, really, by the kind of distribution the product gets.

There are two ways I recommend measuring the impact of marketing:

- Brand Health assessment, which determines the strength of brand equity and awareness
- Performance measurement, which focuses on measuring the impact of marketing tactics and how to improve on them

2. Brand Health Tracking

All brands need a steward. A brand steward nurtures and monitors the health of the brand: its image, positioning, and performance.

Brand health monitoring is a multi-measure undertaking that involves assessing a brand's strengths, in absolute terms, and relative to the competition. It involves knowing how your brand is responding to marketing spend and whether or not to adjust. Brand health monitoring is the simplest form of understanding the impact of your marketing spend on awareness, frequency of usage, and imagery.

Conversion

There is a flow to conversion metrics. That flow aligns with the buyer journey. Since awareness is most often correlated with trial and interest to purchase, it is going to be the most important. No one can buy a product they've never heard of. Awareness converts into consideration. Consideration converts to purchase. Purchase converts to loyalty. And, loyalty converts to advocacy. Most research houses have brand health models with norms and goals for these conversion rates.

Net Promoter Scores (NPS) should be thought of as the vital measure of loyalty and advocacy. This is where the brand's overall positive "likelihood to recommend" percentage is subtracted from the negative "likelihood to recommend" percentage. There are derivatives of this, but this is essentially the basic NPS measurement. The bigger the positive gap, the better.

Equity Assessment

All the hard work translating the brand position into language is measured with equity assessment. Brand equity assessment focuses on perceptions of the brand as measured by movement on key attributes.

It measures the effectiveness of your message principally on:

- Did you do a good job translating your messaging into good content?

- Is what you are saying resonating with customers? Is it driving purchases and loyalty? Is it having an impact on the NPS?

Usually, it takes time for brands to react to marketing spend. The success of those initiatives should be based on sustained changes, not short-term bumps. While brands tend to have small changes on KPIs, the significant movements come with sustained marketing.

It can take as much as six months for brands to move the needle consistently on important brand health measures, even with heavy ad spend. For most brands, it takes a good deal of spend to have an immediate impact on brand health—unless there is a significant event, like a product recall, or money spent on a Super Bowl TV ad.

So, because it is hard to move the needle on KPIs in the short term, running ongoing brand health tracking tends to pick up a lot of small movements and noise in the data that may not be explainable with the existing initiative.

If you want to see how your program impacts equity in the short term, then measure brand health before and after the launch of the program. Measuring it in this way will allow you to more accurately measure the impact of the key attributes that drive purchase, as well as how the marketing spend affected those attributes.

There is an important caveat related to brand health measurement, if you do choose to run an ongoing tracker. Because it is likely that your study will pick up small bumps along the way, it is important to recognize that a small movement on large samples may not be important, even if it is statistically significant.

If you're ever confused, remember McCullough's second law of statistics:

"Never, ever confuse (statistical) significance with importance."

It's been my experience that measuring brand health more than twice a year can be misleading—especially if you are running studies with large sample sizes and reporting small movements.

3. Marketing Return on Investment (MROI)

To really understand the revenue impact of marketing spend and choice of marketing tactics, measure and model the return on your investment.

Marketing ROI models vary, but the basic formula is:

MROI = (Gross Profit – Marketing Investment)/Marketing Investment

Basically, how much money comes back for each dollar spent. There are variations to this formula. Gross profit is most often used internally. However, an alternative would be to measure the return on advertising spend (ROAS) if one were focused purely on whether or not the spending on media is of the greatest interest.

- Understanding MROI helps you know the effectiveness of your marketing spend.
- Knowing the effectiveness of your marketing spend informs how you can modify spend.
- Measuring the impact of your marketing spend year-over-year provides guidance on budget allocation.

- Knowing the effectiveness informs you of the value of each tactic provided in the sales process.

To help understand the importance of measuring MROI, let's look at the following two charts.

The Contribution to Revenue chart is a waterfall chart showing which tactics were responsible for the greatest dollar contribution to revenue.

- The bookends of the chart are the previous and current year-end total revenue for the product.
- In the example below, marketing accounted for $45,000 in revenue.
- Social Media accounted for $20,000; Print: $5,000; and Long-form Digital: $60,000 of the current year total.

Tactics can also have a negative impact on customer spending, like raising prices, driving volume and revenue down.

- In the chart below, you can see how raising prices contributes negatively (-$40,000) to overall revenue.

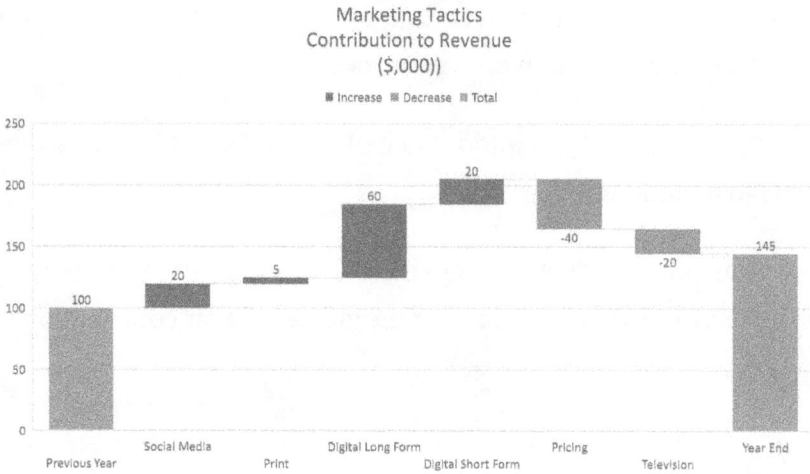

Marketing Tactics
Contribution to Revenue
($,000))

But that's not the *complete* story.

The next chart illustrates the return on investment for each of those marketing tactics.

The total impact on revenue for the marketing program is $.81 per dollar spent. Ideally, though it's not usually the case, you would hope your marketing is effective enough to get a dollar or more back for every dollar spent. Some of these tactics do very well, some less so.

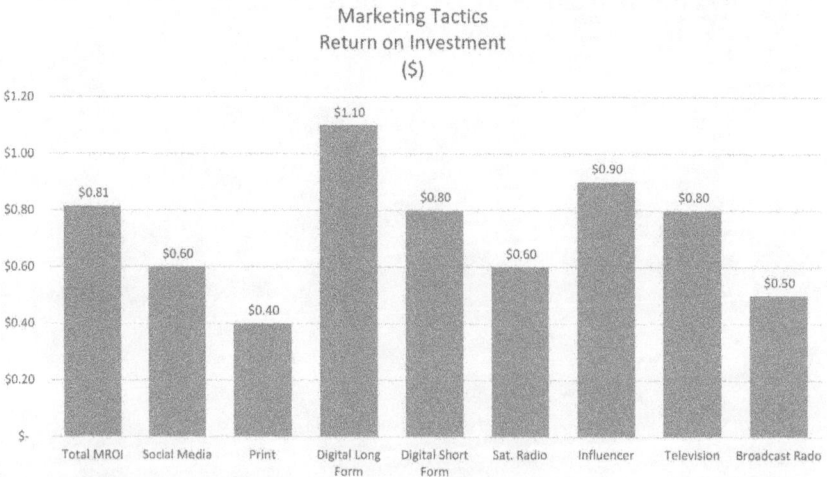

Marketing Tactics
Return on Investment
($)

The combination of these two charts indicates that digital long-form marketing is the most effective way to generate the highest ROI.

However, there is a third aspect to MROI, and it requires taking the above information and looking at it over time. This helps us answer: How much did spending change year over year, and how did that affect the return on investment?

In this next chart, the ROI's are compared year-over-year, with the changes in spending added to the bottom of the chart. Adding spending to the bottom of the chart will help us understand how spending changes may have affected the ROIs.

To make this example simple, this chart illustrates:

- In total, a little bit more was spent, and marketing retained its ROI.
- Social media was a little less effective for the same spend. This would suggest we look at the content to see if it was still fresh and relevant.
- Print went down in effectiveness because the spending was not meaningful enough. It might imply that it would have been best not to spend that money at all.
- Digital long form received further investment, and its effectiveness increased by 50 percent.
- Influencer marketing took hold and became more effective for less spend.

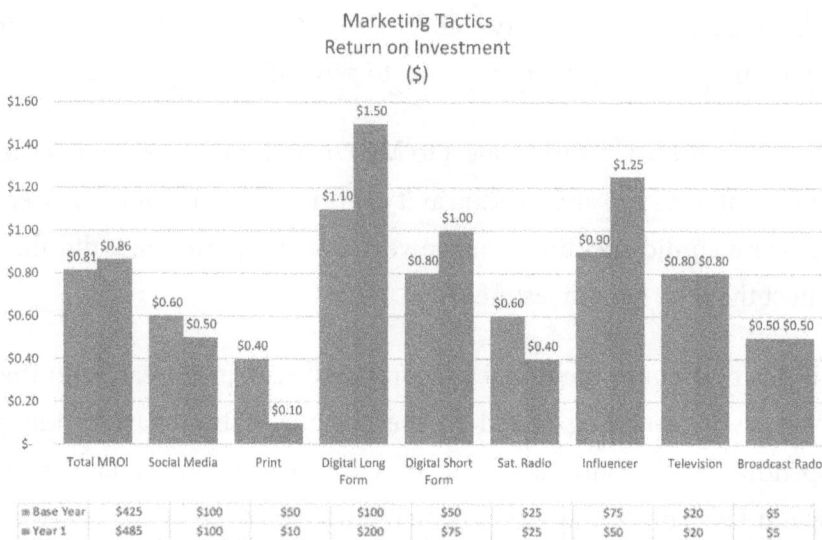

Marketing Tactics
Return on Investment
($)

	Total MROI	Social Media	Print	Digital Long Form	Digital Short Form	Sat. Radio	Influencer	Television	Broadcast Rado
Base Year	$425	$100	$50	$100	$50	$25	$75	$20	$5
Year 1	$485	$100	$10	$200	$75	$25	$50	$20	$5

Waterfall contribution and ROI charts are among the most valuable performance measurement analyses in marketing. And, depending on the product category and if there is enough data, the analysis can be performed quickly.

Purely digital brands, such as Lifelock, can run models and adjust spending on the fly. In businesses where marketing impact lags sales, and sales data takes longer to collect, models are typically run less frequently.

Important Measurement Considerations

Measurement is never as straightforward as you would like. These are complex models and require some understanding of the following constructs:

- Working vs. non-working dollars
- Lagged effects of advertising
- Multi-touch attribution

- A/B testing

Nuances: Working vs. Non-working MROI

I'm only bringing this up because I have been through this more than once.

Finance and marketing teams can be at odds with each other when determining whether to include "non-working" dollars in the ROI calculation. Non-working dollars are the dollars that are not directly used to reach the customer. Marketers will only want to justify their working dollars—the dollars that were used to reach their audience, including the "non-working" dollars that were spent on research and creating the message.

When non-working dollars are included, the impact of early marketing spend will have a lower ROI. Non-working expenses are usually eliminated later on in the execution, and the ROIs would be higher at that point.

If the non-working expenses are spread over the entire program, then the ROI's would be more reflective of the return on the total spend. For instance, if advertising were to run for two years, then the non-working expenses should be spread out over that time.

Since it is difficult to do well and justify, it is usually standard practice to track and compare ROI over time, excluding non-working dollars.

Lagged Effects of Advertising

Every brand's advertising behaves differently because the creative, advertising levels, and frequency vary. But, the principle of lagged effects remains the same: ad spending has an immediate impact the first week and a lasting and diminishing effect over the next four weeks. More importantly, there is a cumulative effect. The spend of the second week overlaps and builds upon the lagged effects of the first week's spend. And the third week's spend overlaps with the diminishing effects of the first week's spend and the diminishing effects of the second week's spend.

The chart below illustrates the sales of one brand received for 100 target rating points (TRPs) in spending. Advertising generated a lift of 6.6% in revenue relative to what would have happened if no advertising were run. In the second week, the lift diminished to just 4.7%, and so on for the twelve weeks plotted. The impact diminished over time but was bolstered by the carryover from the previous week.

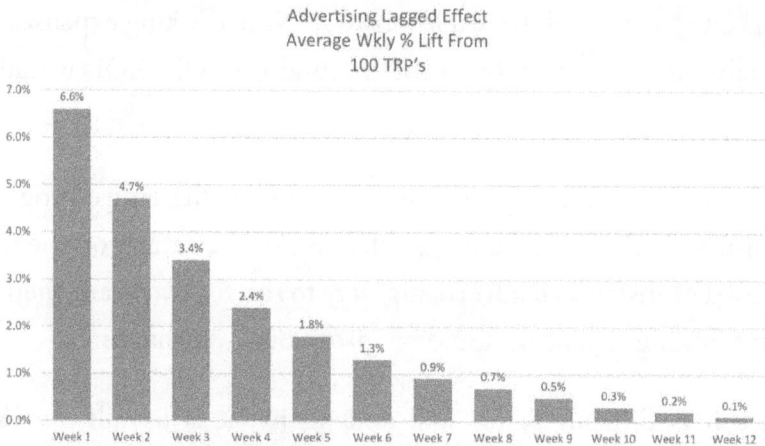

Advertising Lagged Effect
Average Wkly % Lift From
100 TRP's

Note: TRPS's are the percentage of a company's target audience that sees its commercials or advertisements.

The powerful cumulative effect of advertising is one of the reasons why advertising works. The message gets out there and is seen or heard more than once. Then, depending upon its salience, it resonates beyond the first impression. In addition, the second and third and fourth impressions reinforce that effect.

Multi-Touch Attribution

In the early days of marketing analytics, determining which tactic had the most impact wasn't challenging. Television had the most reach. Coupons were in newspapers and were targeted toward coupon clippers. Magazines ads were published less frequently and reached fewer but more targeted people. Radio was broadcast and typically heard in cars. So, there was not too much confusion or overlap in those models. Usually, either the first or the last exposure was the most impactful.

Attributing a purchase to the exposure to a marketing tactic like digital ad spending is more challenging. Digital attribution is so much more difficult because digital marketing shows up just about everywhere.

If a brand is running an integrated marketing campaign in a way where it surrounds the customer with its message on multiple sites with multiple media, it gets much harder to attribute which exposure was the most important in driving a purchase.

It's easier when a customer clicks through from a banner ad and completes the shopping process at the moment. But not everyone engages in impulse buying. What if it takes three views of a banner ad, exposure to an embedded video, and an e-mail campaign to make a sale? How do you account for the impact of each exposure? Even then, a customer may not make a purchase until much later.

This challenge exists in both customer and B2B sales models. In B2B models, it is even more challenging, where the purchase cycle is longer, and the content needs to be consistent and come from multiple sources over a long time.

Here are a few ways to think about how to attribute marketing in a multi-attribute integrated marketing campaign:

- The first touch model gives 100 percent of the credit to the to the first touchpoint a user makes that led to a conversion.

- The last touch model is the simplest model for attribution systems to measure. The final touch gets the most credit.

- Linear measurement distributes impact by evenly applying credit to every touchpoint in the buyer journey.

- Position-based modeling assigns equal impact to the first touch and the one that converted the lead to purchase. The remainder of the impact is spread among the touch points in the middle.

- Custom attribution models differ from vendor to vendor and are the most challenging and time-consuming to build and validate—but they will be the most accurate. At Del Monte and at Big Heart Pet Brands, agent-based modeling combined with survey and behavioral data was the most accurate.

Since the models that work tend to be different from dataset to dataset, it will take some time to find the one that works the best for your data.

A/B Testing

For the purpose of marketing measurement and to see what works, we can simplify this topic. This is pretty straightforward stuff. When working on messaging in the digital space, different executions can be and should be tested very quickly.

A/B testing is one of the easiest and more affordable ways to compare the impact of different messages. Take one execution that you like. Launch it with a sample of your target audience. Then execute an alternative version, again with a different sample of your target audience. It could be a slight modification to the first one, or completely different. Then compare the results to see which worked best.

Marketing technology tools helps do this iteratively and on the fly. They help you zero in on the right content quickly and see what variations will be the most effective.

A/B testing has taken the place of direct research in many places. It is quick and easy, and assuming you have the basis for understanding what is working, you probably don't need to spend time and money on traditional market research to get the answer of what works best.

4. Marketing Measurement

From the very basic brand health assessment to the very sophisticated multi-attribution ROI models, there is no substitute for knowing what is working and what is most effective. It's really the only way to prove that your marketing works to those who might be skeptical. And, it is common sense if you want to be prudent with your budget. To improve decision making and marketing, some level of measurement and diagnostics should be put in place to optimize marketing spend.

CHAPTER 11

"It is the notion that if you carefully think everything through, if you are meticulous and plan well and consider all possible outcomes, you are more likely to create a lasting product.

But I should caution that if you seek to plot out all your moves before you make them—if you put your faith in slow, deliberative planning in the hopes it will spare you failure down the line—well, you're deluding yourself.

For one thing, it's easier to plan derivative work—things that copy or repeat something already out there. So, if your primary goal is to have a fully worked out, set-in-stone plan, you are only upping your chances of being unoriginal. Moreover, you cannot plan your way out of problems.

While planning is very important, and we do a lot of it, there is only so much you can control in a creative environment.

In general, I have found that people who pour their energy into thinking about an approach and insisting that it is too early to act are wrong just as often as people who dive in and work quickly.

The over planners just take longer to be wrong (and, when things inevitably go awry, are more crushed by the feeling that they have failed).

There's a corollary to this, as well: The more time you spend mapping out an approach, the more likely you are to get attached to it. The nonworking idea gets worn into your brain, like a rut in the mud.

It can be difficult to get free of it and head in a different direction. Which, more often than not, is exactly what you must do."

Ed Catmull, Founder Pixar[38]
Excerpt from Creativity, Inc.

Developing a Brilliant Solution to a Nagging Problem

1984

My very first new product test was a 4x6 block of plywood with two-sided adhesive backing on one side and a little metal ring on the other side. The block was the size of a 4x6 photograph. All the consumer had to do was peel back the adhesive and stick the photograph right on the plywood block. In this way, consumers found an easy way to hang a picture on the wall. Not an earth-shattering idea, but the product tested well. Nothing fancy.

In 1992, I was part of the consulting team that worked on the market research for the Apple Newton—quite a different experience from the little block of wood I had tested years before. The Newton was a great idea. Consumers loved the concept. When we tested the product with consumers, the hardware wasn't quite working. So, instead, we ran wires from a "dummy" Newton device to a computer hidden behind a wall so that we could simulate the user experience. Consumers loved it again. But, when the final product was tested with the bugs in the handwriting recognition, product appeal suffered.

In 1998, AT&T had come up with a picture phone that allowed consumers to see the person on the other end of the line. Consumers loved the idea, but in practice, they were not ready to be seen in their pajamas or with hair uncombed. AT&T would have to get more than one person to buy the phone as well. Another challenge that seemed insurmountable. Consumers weren't ready for FaceTime yet.

In 2012, the Milk-Bone team began extensive research to solve the number-one pain point from dog owners—helping their pets live longer. It is a well-known fact that gum disease is a significant barrier to pets living longer, healthier lives. Presented with the concept, pet parents loved the idea of a Milk-Bone treat that helped prevent gum disease. There were other treats on the market that made this claim, but none could really claim efficacy. The Milk-Bone team worked to create a product that the dog would love, and that actually cleaned teeth and prevented gum disease. The idea, the expression, and the product were a hit.

These ideas were well thought out and originated from consumer pain points. Some worked, and some did not, but all of them were tested with consumers to improve upon the idea and validate the scale of the idea.

2013

A note comes from someone in the C-suite, hand-scribbled on some e-mail or article: "Why aren't we doing this…". The attachment has an article about a new product coming to the marketplace.

This was a pretty common occurrence. I had seen this come down from high on up before. Someone from the C-suite would see something they liked or hadn't seen before and wondered why we weren't doing it. Some were reasonable, but mostly not so much.

This one was different. When I was sitting with a VP from my team in my office, she showed me the e-mail from someone in the C-suite, which said something to the effect, "My wife thinks this is a good idea, and we should do it…" This idea was water for dogs.

Ideas for growth can come from unusual places and people, but they're not always good ones.

1. Everything Grows

Everything, whether it is a business or a person, needs to grow. For a business, outside of marketing innovation, real growth typically comes in four areas: category adjacencies, new need territories, new channels of distribution, and bend-the-curve opportunities—those that are disruptive and unseen.

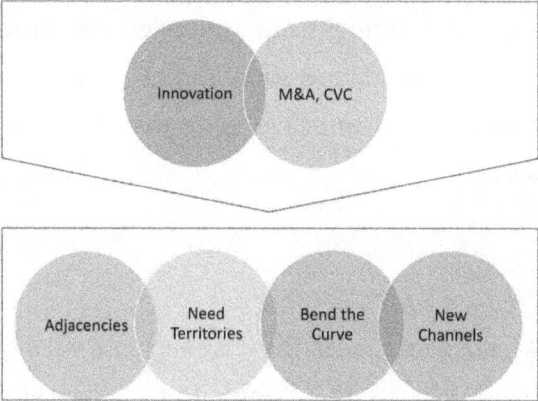

New avenues of growth can originate in your core portfolio and expand to product extensions, then out to new categories and new services.

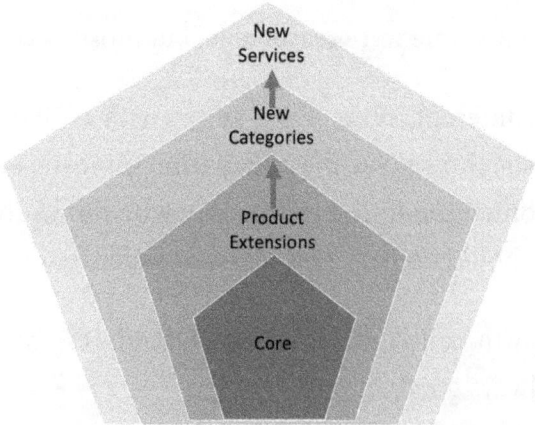

Also, consider how the choices for growth increase dramatically when considering the dimensionality of multiple products, value tiers, or brands in a portfolio.

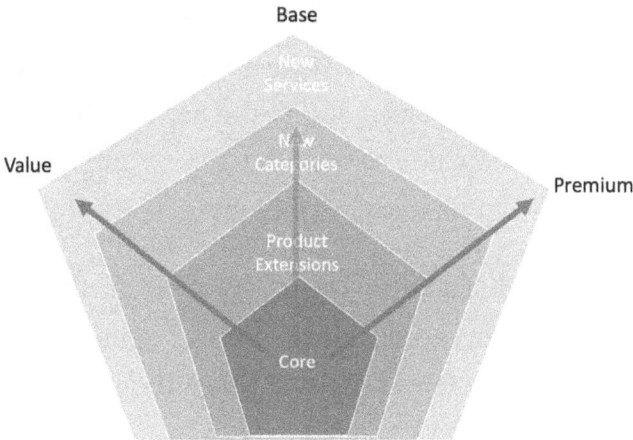

As opportunities move out from the core, the likelihood grows that the time it will take to develop, take hold in the market, and monetize will take longer. Bend-the-curve opportunities typically take longer because you can't see the opportunity yet, to shape it.

2. Time Horizons

Consider how long it takes to develop an idea and bring it to market. The more complex the idea or product, the longer this process takes, and the longer it will take to realize revenue. For pharmaceutical drugs, it can take seven to ten years![39]

When looking for ways to grow, start by examining the purpose of the growth venture, how complex it is, and how long it will take to realize.

Based on the business impact and the time it takes to develop, time horizons are a pretty easy and standard way to categorize innovation.

- **Refresh:** This is a common approach to short-term innovation like product extensions. These ideas typically meet an existing customer need. They are less complicated, fast to develop, do not require rigorous testing, and can hit the market in six to eighteen months.

  They are designed to bolster revenues in the short term and/or support product lines that are lagging. In the product life cycle, they often refresh mature products or brands and extend their life.

  Refreshing a product or line of products replaces the poor performers until a more meaningful portfolio strategy can be developed.

  For a fledgling company, short-term development can bring news to a portfolio that is seeking new funding or looking to increase the breadth of its brand portfolio in the buyer's eyes.

- **Remake:** Medium-term innovation can be somewhat hard to define, especially when things seem to be moving at either 0 or 60 miles per hour.

  Medium-term innovation often occurs in an underdeveloped space. Development time is typically a little longer than a simple line/portfolio extension, and the resources required will be more extensive.

This kind of development can break some new ground, too, and might be used to freshen the portfolio two years later.

The opportunity tends to be more attractive, but the cost of development steeper and the margins a little thinner. In the long run, however, it represents a more meaningful opportunity.

- **Transform:** Transformational innovation seeks to evolve the portfolio based on where you can expect the category to be heading. It should represent the future of the brand and also fit within the defined guardrails. It requires a good deal more thought, resources, and testing, and will test the resolve and patience of the developers and company. It extends the horizon by looking at white spaces that may not be fully understood yet by customers. The story of their value has yet to be told or appreciated.

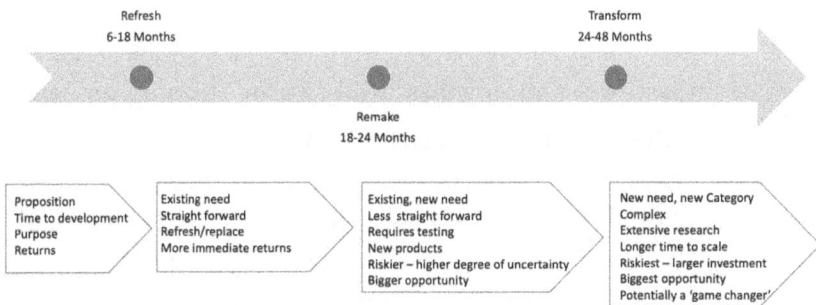

Refresh
6-18 Months

Transform
24-48 Months

Remake
18-24 Months

Proposition	Existing need	Existing, new need	New need, new Category
Time to development	Straight forward	Less straight forward	Complex
Purpose	Refresh/replace	Requires testing	Extensive research
Returns	More immediate returns	New products	Longer time to scale
		Riskier – higher degree of uncertainty	Riskiest – larger investment
		Bigger opportunity	Biggest opportunity
			Potentially a 'game changer'

The mix of short-, medium-, and long-term innovation depends upon the resolve and resources of the organization. The mix may change over time, but it is aligned to the long-term brand strategy.

3. Platforms

Platforms are another way of thinking about how to structure growth. Platforms can serve as the foundation for a stream of products to follow. The best platforms are those that allow innovation to be multidimensional.

- If your platform is diabetes health, for example, you can look at expansion platforms like food, testing supplies, and wellness services. For instance, there are simple and straightforward low-sugar products that people with diabetes integrate into their everyday lives. Then there are meal kit services, like Diet-To-Go, that offer diabetic-friendly meal delivery kits. Those are two vertical markets into which one company can entertain entering. CVS and Walgreens offer testing kits. The idea that they could support their diabetic community with access to partnership services that support meals does not seem like a stretch.

- Swiffer went from a simple floor duster to a wet mop to a blinds duster and now has products for cleaning up behind pets. Roomba has evolved similarly.

- A pet food company looking to innovate might launch a new flavor. Then it might enter a new category, like dog treats. Then it might move into services like offering pet insurance, pet hotels, or dog walking services. By extending into other product categories and services, the company embeds itself more deeply into the lives of the customer.

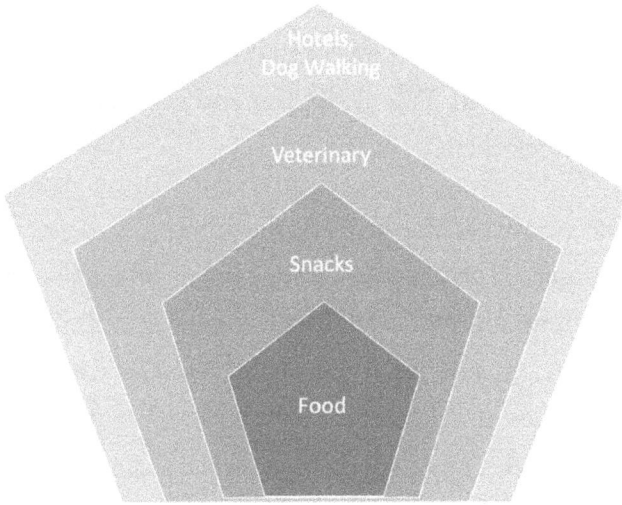

Mars Pet Care expanded their portfolio by adding premium food brands like Innova, Banfield veterinary services, and Whistle GPS tracking collar devices for dogs.

- One of the most successful customer platforms is the pod technology employed by both Nespresso and Keurig. The hardware is the solution, but the growth is in the ability to add different coffees and flavors, and even license out to different brands. Using the coffee pod platform enables brands to reach new customers that they might not have otherwise been able to.

- Just think about all the products that have spun off from Tide Detergent. The original core product was introduced in 1946 in powder form. Over the years, it has extended the product to liquid form and launched specialized products for improved odor control such as a Sport line and worked with other internal brands like Febreze to launch a co-branded product. Then came the new product categories, like the pen stain removers and then Tide Pods. Tide has also moved into services with its Tide Dry Cleaners, a test concept available in some markets.

- Take a look at the grocery shopping and delivery service Instacart. Grocers see home meal kits as competitors encroaching on their business. A major nationwide grocery chain might just buy a company like Instacart to gain the efficiencies of delivering meals, as well as foods, in an effort to boost sales and meet a consumer need gap they don't yet support.

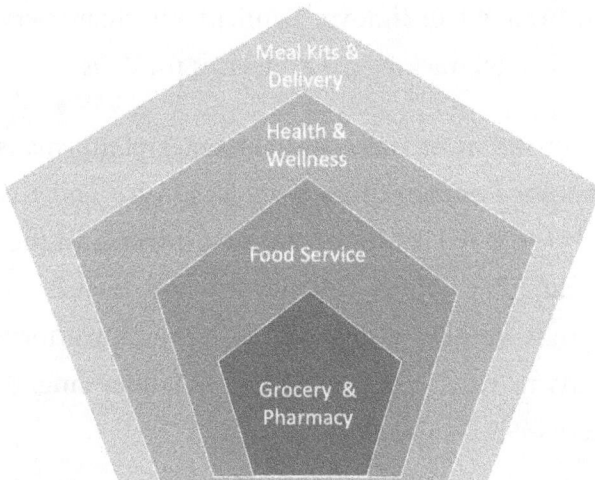

- IKEA purchased Task Rabbit to make it easier for their customers to achieve easy assembly of the notoriously challenging furniture IKEA sells.

4. M&A for Growth

Relative to internal innovation, the opportunity for M&A to drive transformational growth can be more substantial and take less time. Additionally, M&A can build scale through brand extensions and portfolio expansion. It might even be more affordable, given the number of resources required to develop internally.

It is not uncommon for brands to seek acquisitions of other brands, technologies, and capabilities to increase speed to market and extend the business into new categories. Cherry-picking great ideas from the world of start-ups in any space—from tech to consumables—can extend a customer base, portfolio, and revenue, improve operations, and talent pool. M&A and corporate ventures have become so hot precisely for this reason.

Amazon, Google, and Apple have led the way in acquiring talent and ideas through the acquisition of start-ups. CPG has been acquiring new food and beverage ideas at a rapid pace. PepsiCo, Unilever, and General Mills are a few of the many who are actively seeking growth opportunities through this lens.

Every mature company wants to buy a young (unicorn) company that's going to rejuvenate its business. Every young company wants to be that unicorn—or the company with a private market value of over $1 billion.

Global M&A activity among the world's top 50 customer goods companies—from Procter & Gamble and L'Oréal to Nestle and Unilever—jumped 45% to a 15-year high of 60 deals in 2017.[40]

Over the last ten years, Kellogg's has acquired 14 companies. This strategy doesn't always work out, though. In Kellogg's case, it bought Keebler Foods in 2000 for $3.9 billion and then in 2019 sold it for $1.3 billion.

By comparison, General Mills has acquired about 17 companies over the last 10 years and divested 5 companies. Its largest purchase was in 2000 when it bought Pillsbury for $10.5 billion.[41]

5. The M&A Filters

Portfolio Architecture

Regardless of how growth occurs, whether through innovation or M&A, how you build and organize your portfolio of products matters.

House of Brands

A House of brands strategy is when the corporate brand is the umbrella under which multiple brands live. The brands may or may not be related. Each has its own identity. Though they should always be connected to the broader corporate mission, they do not need to be connected to each other.

P&G is the perfect example of a house of brands, as is General Mills and the JM Smucker Company. Big Heart Pet Brands was a house of brands. Mostly, the brands in their portfolios do not halo back, positively or negatively, on the parent brand.

Big Heart Pet Brands, shown below, had at least nine brands in its portfolio.

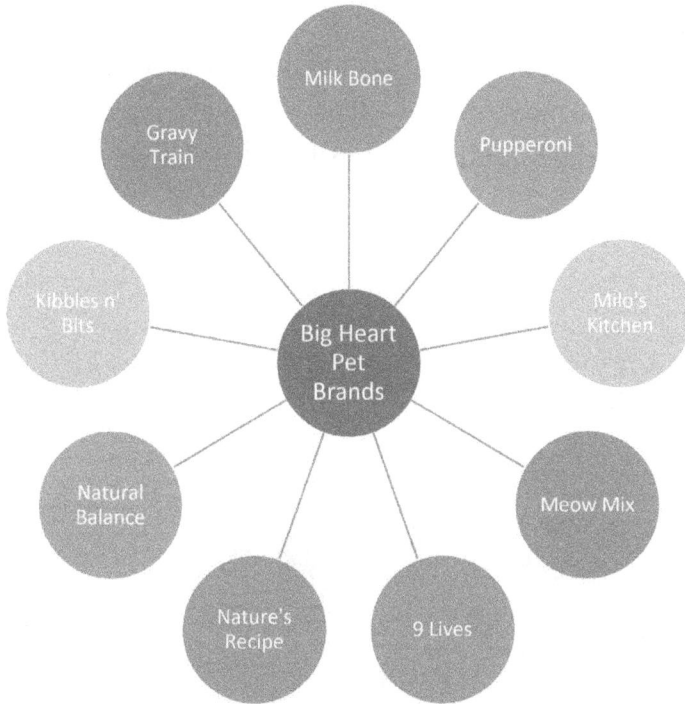

Milk Bone

Gravy Train

Pupperoni

Kibbles n' Bits

Milo's Kitchen

Big Heart Pet Brands

Natural Balance

Meow Mix

Nature's Recipe

9 Lives

None of these brands are connected to one another. Nor are they linked to the higher brand identity of Big Heart Pet Brands. Retailers and brand marketing would work together across all of these brands. Still, the end user never was made aware of the linkage—principally because of the varying health credentials of each product and the lack of an identity of the parent brand.

Endorsed Brands and Hybrid Structures

Hybrid structures and endorsed branding strategy allow individual brands to benefit from the supportive role of the larger parent brand. Like the House of Brands strategy, the brands themselves are allowed to build their equities, all the while benefiting from the overall portfolio and brand halo.

Marriott is the most commonly cited example of a master brand that has quite a few endorsed sub-brands, but most of these do little to halo back to the master brand. Marriott also has stand-alone brands like Ritz Carlton, and Marriott-branded hotels like the JW Marriott.[42]

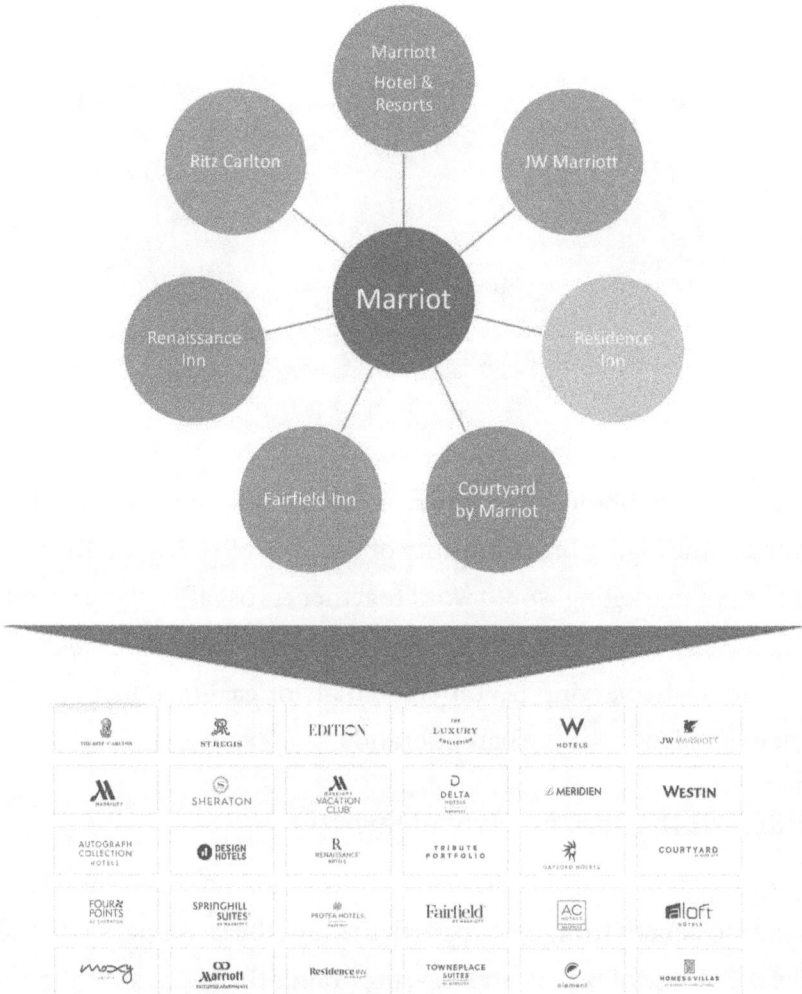

Few customers are likely to think of Alphabet, Google's parent company, in the same way as they think of Google. The Alphabet hybrid structure has stand-alone brands like Verily Life Sciences and Waymo, and an endorsed corporate brand structure as well. Google's brand name is attached to the Google Cloud, the Google Pixel phone, Google Home, Google Mail, Google Earth, and more.[43]

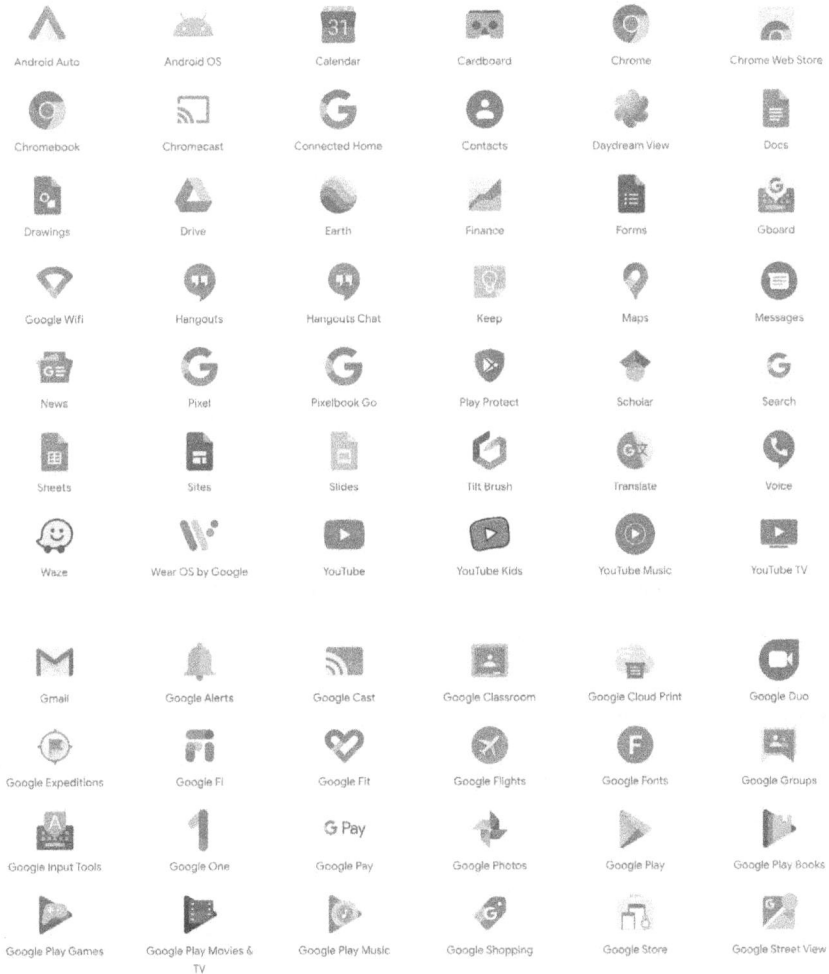

Android Auto	Android OS	Calendar	Cardboard	Chrome	Chrome Web Store
Chromebook	Chromecast	Connected Home	Contacts	Daydream View	Docs
Drawings	Drive	Earth	Finance	Forms	Gboard
Google Wifi	Hangouts	Hangouts Chat	Keep	Maps	Messages
News	Pixel	Pixelbook Go	Play Protect	Scholar	Search
Sheets	Sites	Slides	Tilt Brush	Translate	Voice
Waze	Wear OS by Google	YouTube	YouTube Kids	YouTube Music	YouTube TV
Gmail	Google Alerts	Google Cast	Google Classroom	Google Cloud Print	Google Duo
Google Expeditions	Google Fi	Google Fit	Google Flights	Google Fonts	Google Groups
Google Input Tools	Google One	Google Pay	Google Photos	Google Play	Google Play Books
Google Play Games	Google Play Movies & TV	Google Play Music	Google Shopping	Google Store	Google Street View

Branded House

A branded house is simply where the corporate brand is on the name of every product in the portfolio. The corporation is the brand. GE is a B2B branded house, with GE Capital, GE Digital, GE Aviation, GE Healthcare, GE Money, and GE Energy underneath the GE brand name.

Federal Express is the classic example:[44]

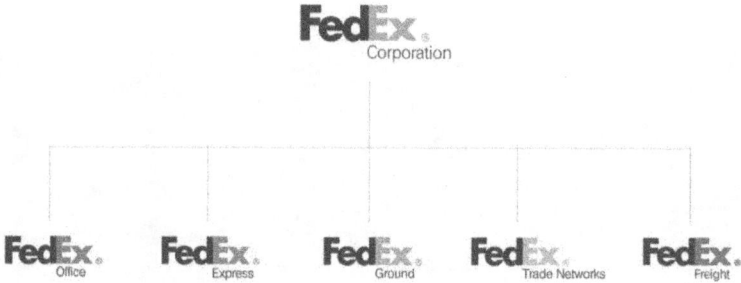

In the other structures, brands compete for resources. In a branded house, most every product within the portfolio benefits from the marketing dollars spent.

Beyond Structure

Brand Awareness, Point of Differentiation, and Fit are three key lenses to consider when doing M&A.

- Awareness: If you are considering acquiring a brand, think about the level of brand penetration. If the acquisition target is a start-up or has low brand awareness, how much work will it take to get traction for this new brand? Will awareness be a barrier to reach new customers? If so, it may be counter-productive to fold an acquisition under your existing brand name.

- Points of Differentiation: Products under consideration should be different from those in the existing portfolio. A product under consideration should extend the current portfolio. It should reach a new, attractive, and profitable audience. Alternatively, provide a unique platform from which you can innovate. For instance, it might bring technology that helps your existing portfolio extend into new places, channels, or categories. If it is going to compete for resources, it might hurt the development of other brands.

- Portfolio Fit: New product acquisitions should fit with the brand identity of your existing portfolio. It's not critical, but if it doesn't, it should have a good reason to stand on its own. Does the actual product make sense in your portfolio? It should not cannibalize on your existing business. The best of all worlds is that an acquisition provides you with a portfolio that is cohesive and seamless from one product to the next.

6. Buying Growth

With some businesses, their typical first choice for how to grow is through acquisition. JM Smuckers has done this with Big Heart Pet Brands, Sahale Snacks, Folgers Coffee, and more. That's because sometimes it is far easier to buy your way into a new market than to build or innovate successfully within the company.

For decades, PepsiCo and Coca Cola's M&A activity had focused mainly on filling gaps in their product portfolio to match customer needs, rather than innovating within. In the early 2000s, customer preferences moved away from sugary carbonated beverages. They wanted drinks with vitamins and minerals.

At the time, PepsiCo was focusing on giving itself a foothold into the rapidly growing non-carbonated beverage sector. Sobe Beverages was one of the first brands to promise to deliver functional benefits from an innovative ingredient composition, like Ginseng, Guarana, and Black Tea. In 2006, the company bought Naked Juice and Izze to expand its juice offerings. In 2016, in response to the influence of the gut biome trend, Pepsi bought Kevita, which makes fermented probiotic and kombucha beverages.

7. Growth through Corporate Venture

Incubation and Acceleration

Corporate Venture Capital (CVC) is similar to M&A and continues to grow in popularity as a means to find new growth. The nature of CVC is essentially investing and testing the waters before acquiring another firm.

From 2011 to 2016[45], there were over 421 new corporate venture capital arms created. According to CB Insights, in 2018, there were 2,740 deals worth over $53 billion.[46]

The rapid growth in accelerators resembles that of a Wild West gold rush (or if you prefer, the dot.com era) as people look to invest and/or look for funding. Pitch events are everywhere and are typically organized by incubator and accelerator programs. In their 2016 accelerator report, the fundraising management platform, Gust, identified over 10,000 accelerators globally. For some perspective, just five years ago, another study (Get2Growth) placed the total number of accelerated start-ups ever at just around 3,000 from less than 200 accelerators.[47]

Every major city has at least one established accelerator/incubator program, sometimes multiple. Some incubators, like PlugandPlay-TechCenter (located in San Francisco), serve the tech industry, and offer traditional incubator support services like access to financing, program classes, and events. Others, like Rocketspace, are more focused on providing a coworking space for any young entrepreneurially minded start-up.

Incubators often boast about their contribution to the economy. The San Francisco-based food incubator, Kitchentown, for example, claims to have helped over 421 companies, created over 367 jobs, and helped secure over $52 million in funding.[48]

Crowdfunding platforms like Kickstarter help start-ups source funding from the general public as well as more traditional funding sources.

Lightning doesn't always strike. For every success in venture capital, there are around seven failures. Analyst firm CB Insights did a post mortem on over a thousand US seed tech companies and placed them in a funding round funnel.[49] Of those companies that are able to attract their first round of funding, 38% will fail before they even get to the second round. In total, around 68% of companies that first seek funding fail. It shows just how hard that dream is.

So, when hoping to be the next unicorn or finding the next unicorn, there are no guarantees. The appeal of expanding capabilities, talent, and portfolio reach can be tantalizing.

Consider the case of Natura Pet products. Higher-credential products like Innova and Evo were darling high-credential brands, desired and acquired but eventually sunset by P&G.

On the other hand, Nestle acquired Merrick Dog Food products, with a high-credential line of pet products that extended Nestle's reach into new market niches and customer bases.

8. Innovation Strategy

It's vital for a company to articulate an innovation strategy. There isn't a one-size-fits-all approach. And, while some companies are true innovation leaders, others choose to be followers. Some will build internally. Others will buy it.

As I've tried to illustrate, paths to innovation within a company are wide open. Brands can innovate along a product line or a category or a service. But the goal is to continue to push the boundaries to innovate well beyond today—to be prepared for the future.

If you innovate internally, what are the strengths you will leverage to win with innovation? Your innovation strategy needs to lay out a support structure—one that takes into consideration culture, process, skill sets, and testing.

9. The Culture of Innovation

The culture of innovation means providing a creative space to innovate. This translates to:

1. Organizational commitment to the process
2. The space to create—both physically and intellectually

Commitment to the Process

A real culture of innovation means leadership involvement, resources, and patience. Developing a culture of innovation can be hard when the innovation team is under the microscope to produce. Whether it be for quarterly results, fiscal responsibility to keep the doors open, or a demanding C-suite, patience means looking beyond the next fiscal quarter.

Leadership commitment means having the C-suite as part of the creation process. Having the CEO involved shows the organization is committed to innovation, but even more importantly, it minimizes questions farther down the road when it is too late to make corrections.

Some CEOs may not want to be involved. In that case, at a minimum, build a feedback loop to help guide product development. Periodically building in touchpoints helps with go/no-go decisions farther down the road. When those tight decisions need to be made, no one will be able to claim ignorance.

Physical Space

Companies like Booz Allen Hamilton are creating innovation centers separate from their main offices (to avoid distraction) that provide a place to test, showcase, and measure new concepts.

Big Heart Pet Brands created an innovation space that included many of the design principles executed at IDEO. These included:

- Multi-media conference rooms
- Comfortable seating throughout
- Team/group shared cubicle space to promote co-creation and conversation
- State-of-the-art technology, including 3D printers

Teams need to see that the company is committed to innovation. These innovation centers can be counter-productive if they are created in name only, such as when a company decides to re-paint a few walls in bold colors, install an open floor plan, and add a ping pong table.

Some companies take these measures thinking that they are tools of innovation. Having the creative space isn't just important in a physical sense; it's important in the metaphorical sense that employees have space (or room) to succeed and fail.

Patience

That said, too much can be expected from innovation. In many companies, if a new initiative can't achieve break even on the investment quickly or, even better, generate incremental revenues in the first twelve months, many executives will lose patience and kill the initiative. Even good products can be terminated before they have a chance to find a home in the marketplace.

Over on Wikipedia, the list of discontinued Google products and services is starting to approach the size of the active products and services listed. There are entire sites dedicated to discontinued Google products, like killedbygoogle.com, The Google Cemetery, and didgoogleshutdown.com.

In response to the lack of corporate patience that results in short innovation cycles, many companies have moved to a model of launch and fix later.

Driven initially by software and mobile phones, launches can have flaws that are remedied while still in the market with new software revisions. Rather than have early beta users and testing, the entire marketplace has become the place for identifying areas of improvement.

Some will see this as a form of strategic product marketing, a way of figuring out what works faster by getting the product to market to get validation as quickly as possible. In contrast, others recognize that the frequent culling of products has the potential to damage a brand that requires trust and investment.

10. The Process

In a CB Insights study, more than 8 in 10 corporate CEOs said that innovation was extremely or very important to their growth strategy. Still, only 4 in 10 said they had well-established innovation processes.[50]

In *The Start-up of You*, Reid Hoffman, founder of LinkedIn, says, "A product won't make money if customers don't want or need it, regardless of how slick its form or function."[51]

When CB Insights conducted its start-up post-mortem, it looked at the reason why products or start-ups failed. The top reason—present in 4 out of 10 failures—was because there was no market need.[52]

When you study the customers long enough, you understand their likes, pain points, and needs. Born from these are new products and services, new ways to package those products and services that create new value for the customer.

Know your customer and their needs, tap into your creativity to develop new products and services that meet their needs, and in doing so, you'll produce outstanding work and unique value to the customer.

Stage-Gate Process

If you are part of a corporate innovation team, you may be familiar with the stage-gate process. This is the process that takes innovation from opportunity identification, development, creation, testing, and validation through to commercialization. It is deliberate and designed to mitigate missteps and create opportunities for improvement in innovation.

The stage gates allow you to re-evaluate ideas because, at each stage, you are engaging with the customer and learning more to optimize the concept. You'll also have the chance to cut ideas before you over-invest. Some ideas just may not be worth pursuing.

Some stage-gate processes are rigid. Innovation is an iterative process that requires the flexibility to pivot if an idea isn't working quite right. So, I prefer to allow for free flow through the creation phases.

Standard Stage-Gate Process

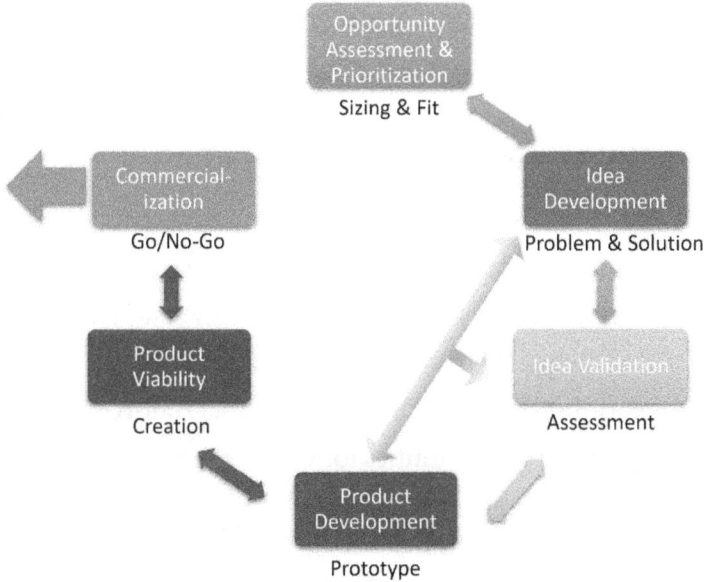

The stage-gate process should free the innovator to think as far out of the box as possible, and then allow for the process to cull the ideas down to the few that will succeed.

Let me just remind you of the Ed Catmull quote at the beginning of the chapter. Over-planners can be wrong. Some may feel like the stage-gate process is over planning. It certainly doesn't guarantee success. But it does help create order in the chaos of innovation and increases the chances of succeeding.

If you are looking at transformation, this model might feel limiting. When pushing transformational ideas through the stage-gate process, those potential customers may not be able to see the brilliance or the benefit of the product you are creating. To adjust for that, provide as much latitude as possible to the innovators within the process.

I believe in the process, no matter how far out the ideas. The farther out the idea, the more creative you have to be in each stage.

Opportunity Assessment and Prioritization

Opportunity assessment can happen at different points, and sometimes multiple points, in the growth process. I spoke of growth opportunities in the macro forces and strategy chapters, as well as earlier in this chapter. Usually, market forces are accelerators and provide fuel for innovation. For instance, a macro force on fair trade drove new sourcing opportunities for Coffees, Teas, Beans, and Acai.

Opportunities may also arise from the SWAT analysis, suggesting leveraging a technology strength in the creation of plant-based packaging instead of plastic.

Or, just by observing consumption trends, uncovering opportunities for growth may arise in categories like water in the late 90s, alternative juices in early 2000's, and now with kombuchas and pre/probiotics.

If you were in finance, you would have recognized a trend toward a desire for greater control over money personal finance. The white space opened up with the introduction of Quicken, then decades later new opportunities opened up for Mint, Credit Karma, and NerdWallet.

All these opportunities need to be examined with the customer in mind—taking a step back to look at macro forces and trends, then overlaying the attitudes, needs, and behaviors of your target audience.

This style of opportunity assessment helps articulate the vision and assess market appeal. Go one step farther and examine how it fits from a strategic perspective.

Consider this way of looking at the assessment process.

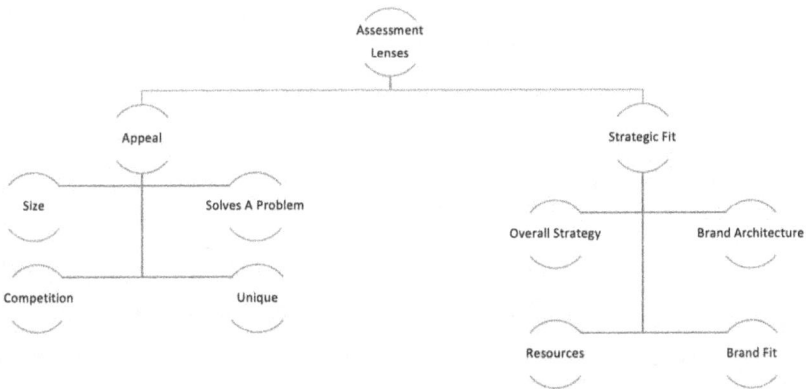

Market Appeal

The market appeal is measured on multiple dimensions.

- Size of the opportunity: How big is the market? What is the revenue potential? Is it growing? Is it local, national, global? If it is emerging, what other comparable markets can you use as benchmarks to model growth?

New product adoption is hard to predict, but market analogs in similar categories can be helpful to triangulate what might happen with new product growth.

It can be as simple as using syndicated sources to get total category sizing. Then add some back-of-the-envelope math to see what might work. For instance, an internet streaming service came to me looking to conduct a market sizing for a niche opportunity. We applied basic market demographics to size the universe, pulled additional data from available sources from Pew research, did a little math, and came up with back-of-the-envelope market sizing.

- <u>The degree to which it solves a customer problem</u>: Does it provide a solution to a customer need? Throwing products into the market without focusing on the customer is pointless. Look at how interested customers are in getting help with their problems.

The new product innovation failure numbers are overwhelming. The Nike Fuel Band was an exciting new product that only reached about 10 percent of the market during the first two years.[53]

- <u>The degree to which the opportunity is unique</u>: Uniqueness is a key new product predictor in most success models. Uniqueness is in the eye of the beholder. But, the product you are providing must be different from the solutions already in the marketplace. If you are not going to be unique, and are planning to follow in the wake of another successful competitor, then the market has to be big enough, and you will need to offer other benefits or a lower price.

Dropbox works very hard to differentiate itself from Google and Apple's cloud service by offering a more collaborative offering rather than just storage, as well as different pricing structures.

Centralize team content

Create, store, and share cloud content from Google Docs, Sheets, and Slides, Microsoft Office files, and Dropbox Paper alongside traditional files in Dropbox.

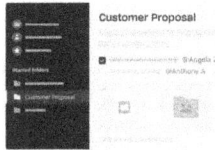

Transform your folders

Dropbox Spaces brings your files and cloud content together, so that your PowerPoints can live next to your Google Docs, Trello boards, and whatever tools your team wants to use.

Team collaboration, any time, anywhere

Easily access your team's work from your computer, mobile device, or any web browser.

Source: DropBox Website[54]

- <u>The nature of the competition:</u> The assessment of competition needs to include a number of metrics to determine the degree to which you'll have to support the brand once launched.

  o Is the market crowded? Are there many players? Is there room in the market for more players?

  o Is it dominated by a monolith (e.g., 70-percent market share)?

  o Does competition have deep pockets? How will they respond to a new entrant?

When you assess an opportunity, it's helpful to think about the relative size. Does your idea exist within a local $10 million market? Or global $10 billion markets? Quantifying the opportunity allows you to see if the insights really have the potential to represent a significant business opportunity.

When you're done, you will be able to rank the opportunities. Visualize them mapping them out on a calendar. What lenses matter most to you? How significant are the opportunities? Do they line up with the strategic initiatives that the company is trying to achieve?

Strategic Fit

Like market appeal, the fit should be examined through multiple lenses.

- Fit with corporate strategy: Going back to the SWAT analysis and marketing plans, ask yourself: How does this opportunity fit with that strategy? How does it meet with existing growth targets?

  What kind of resources do you have to support new opportunities? Do you have enough people? Enough marketing dollars? Distribution? Can you make it?

  Fit with corporate strategy is about as important as it gets. After sizing and appeal, if it doesn't fit with plans, it probably won't get the resources it will need to succeed.

- Fit with master brand equity: The next aspect to consider is fit with master brand equity. The strength and synergy of that relationship will work if there is consistency among the brands.

Does the master brand provide a brand equity halo for a new brand? If the new opportunity provides a positive halo back to the master brand, even better.

Sometimes, acquiring a new brand with a sharp image will refresh older brands or spin them into a more positive light.

Such is the case with many of the corporate sustainability acquisitions, where a new brand is acquired to modernize and make the master brand more socially acceptable.

Visually, then, you can go through a reasonably ordered decision-making process to assess the likelihood of success for each opportunity. If you want to get into more depth, you can give each one more weight. For instance, you can assign more weight to size, resources, or another lens, to reflect the importance of those aspects to the success of the opportunities.

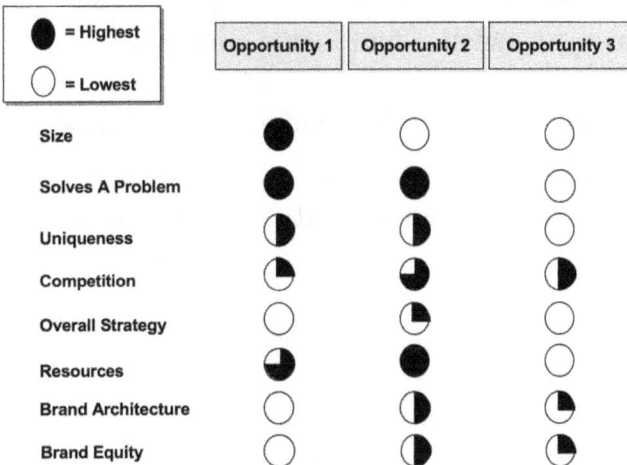

● = Highest
○ = Lowest

	Opportunity 1	Opportunity 2	Opportunity 3
Size	●	○	○
Solves A Problem	●	●	○
Uniqueness	◐	◐	○
Competition	◕	◕	◐
Overall Strategy	○	◕	○
Resources	◕	●	○
Brand Architecture	○	◐	◕
Brand Equity	○	◐	◕

It is still a bit of a subjective scoring system. Take each one and score it. Add up the points at the end. Plot opportunities on a timeline.

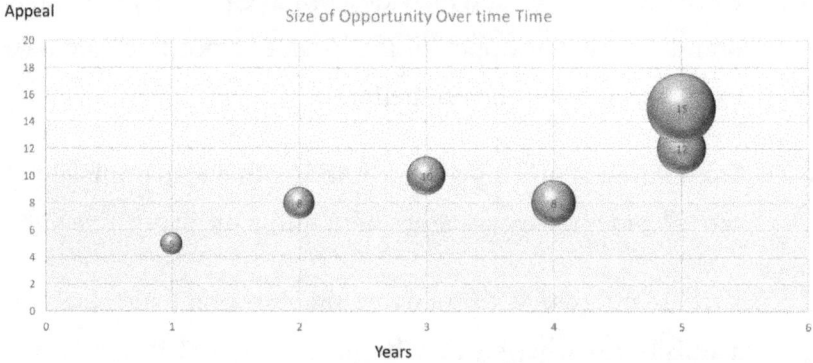

Note: The size of the circle represents the size of the opportunity

11. Idea Development

Think Like a Designer

Thinking like a designer will transform the way organizations develop products, services, processes, and strategies. There are so many companies and universities teaching design thinking that it has become the foundation for modern innovation.

Take a look at the beverage illustration below. You can learn a lot about design thinking by studying the beverage industry and how it has evolved based on customer needs/benefits sought.

1950 ──────────────────────────────▶ 2020					
Evolving Consumer Needs	Refreshment Basic Functionality	Pick Me Up Social/Fun Healthy Alternative	Flavorful Health Portable Hydration Purifying	Fortified Fuel Mood Enhancement Natural &Good For You	Mission Driven New Origins Mental Performance Relaxation Plant Based Energy Sugar as Enemy
Product Evolution	CSD Juice Milk Coffee	RTD Tea RTD Juice	Bottled Water RTD Coffee Wellness Juices & Teas	Isotonics Energy Drinks Fortified Waters Functional Beverages	Sustainably Sourced Organic Everything Cold Pressed Coffee Everything Kombucha Nori, Moringa, etc. CBD Greens Nootropics Alt Sweeteners

Notice how, over time, customer problems/needs changed, and then notice how the industry responded to those needs. It is a fascinating evolution from simple refreshment to the fractional needs that involve purpose, energy, hydration, and mental performance.

In the last two decades, not only is the beverage category focusing on an expanded list of ingredients, but it is explicitly focusing on the benefits delivered by those ingredients and less on the ingredients themselves.

This expanded list of functional benefits includes sleep, cognitive performance, and mood management.

Design Thinking

IDEO, an award-winning global design firm that has been at the forefront of design thinking, described the process as "pulling together what is desirable from a human point of view with what is technologically feasible and economically viable."[55]

The goal is to look at a problem or topic from all angles to see where customer hacks occur—identifying the issues that are so bothersome that people create their own solutions because no solutions exist. Their solutions may not be earth-shattering, but rather small improvements that illustrate a person's resolve to fix a problem.

No matter how you approach it, design thinking is an iterative, multi-step process rooted in empathizing with target users and their pain points.

Human Factors

Empathizing means understanding customers' challenges, needs, solves, and hacks. Interviewing, observing, and spending time with them in their day-to-day lets you get underneath what is going on in their lives. Consider the following tools and techniques to do just that:

Direct Methods

- Brand Enthusiasts: Interviews with brand fanatics capture their passion and the relationships between customers and their favorite brands—how they were forged, and how to maintain them.

- Deprivation Diaries: Most customers can't articulate their love for the products and brands they use every day. Asking customers to do without their favorite products for a while and having them record their daily lives and emotions provides a deeper understanding of the functional and emotional roles specific products play in customers' lives.

- Day-in-the-Life: There's nothing quite like walking a mile in a customer's shoes. Customer-led "tours" of their daily activities and behaviors provide an understanding of what happens in customers' homes and lives. It's illuminating to watch them solve problems with unique hacks. For instance, I've seen pet parents struggle carrying heavy pet food bags from the store to their car, and from their car to the house, and then emptying that bag into a plastic trash can to keep critters at bay.

- Shadowing and Shop-a-longs: Similarly, accompanying customers as they shop stores and exploring their interactions with brands and products in context can show how they look at products, compare products, and make decisions.

- There are some people whose job is to take pictures of shelf sets for clients. Observing, comparing, and filming your product's potential competitive sets on display shelves is a unique way to learn about in-store competitive messaging, promotions, and pricing.

A Day in the Life

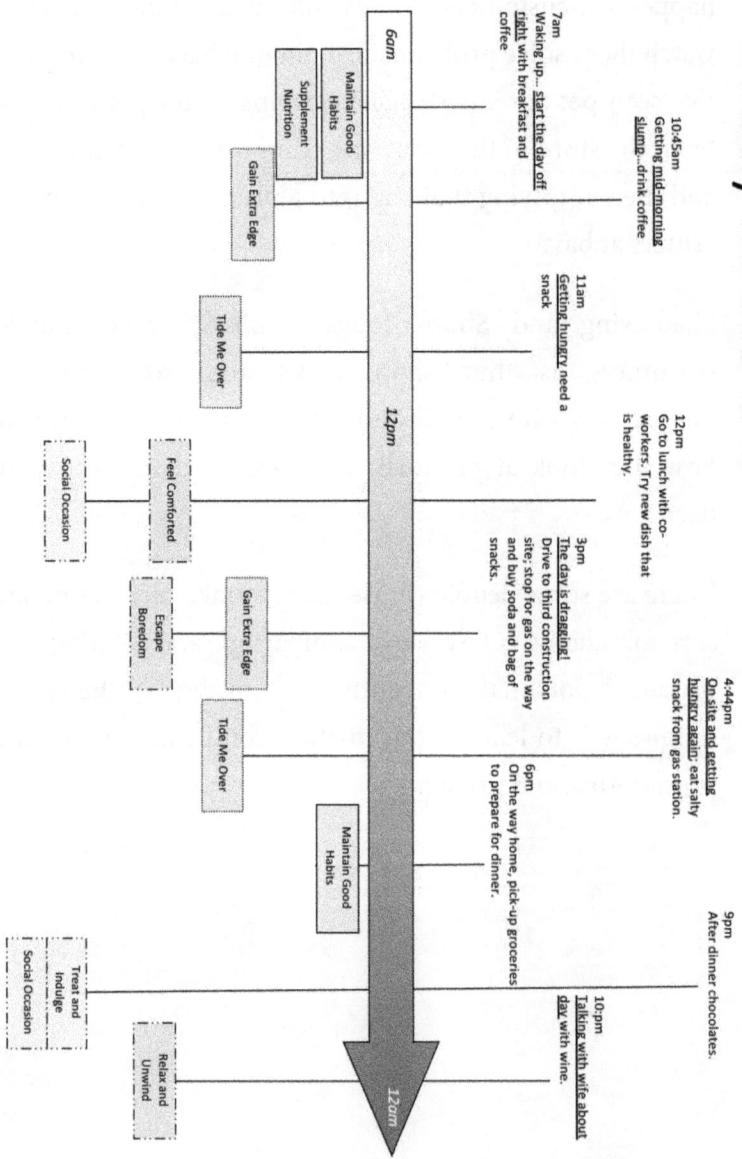

6am

7am
Waking up... start the day off right with breakfast and coffee

- Maintain Good Habits
- Supplement Nutrition

10:45am
Getting mid-morning slump...drink coffee

- Gain Extra Edge

11am
Getting hungry need a snack

- Tide Me Over

12pm

12pm
Go to lunch with co-workers. Try new dish that is healthy.

- Feel Comforted
- Social Occasion

3pm
The day is dragging! Drive to third construction site; stop for gas on the way and buy soda and bag of snacks.

- Gain Extra Edge
- Escape Boredom

4:44pm
On site and getting hungry again; eat salty snack from gas station.

- Tide Me Over

6pm
On the way home, pick-up groceries to prepare for dinner.

- Maintain Good Habits

9pm
After dinner chocolates.

10pm
Talking with wife about day with wine.

- Treat and Indulge
- Social Occasion
- Relax and Unwind

12am

Indirect Methods

- Observation: Observing how consumers use products or shop a store from a distance can give you a slightly different insight than a shop-along. When you walk with a person, their behavior may be a little different than when you are just observing them.

  One of my favorite studies was a theater study, where we hid cameras throughout the lobby of the theater to watch the flow of traffic, body language, and behavior. Route trackers mapped how people moved throughout the lobby and how much time theatergoers spent in each location.

  It turned out, long before they left their house, theatergoers were stressed out about missing the movie. They were worried about start times, missing trailers, not getting the best seats, and wait times in concessions. Many even skipped concessions (the theater's most profitable business) just to make sure they didn't miss anything. Many times, theatergoers would just sit in the theater and wait while only the local ads were displayed on the screen—making the experience worse. Patron boredom was the reason for the addition of high-production-value advertising being shown before the main attraction.

- Expert Interviews: Experts have a broad perspective of the world, the culture, and the categories in which you are interested. They are a great first stop to learn the ins and outs of an unfamiliar category quickly. Most innovation firms make this the first step in most of their research.

GLG is a company that keeps a roster of experts across a wide range of categories and disciplines to help provide expert insight into select topics. Private equity firms make this a first step to learn about a category or brand in which they are interested in investing. Interviewing experts both inside and outside of your category while triangulating them with the macro forces will add to your foundational understanding.

- Cultural Immersions: This kind of exposure immerses those responsible for innovation into different sub-cultures. Whether it be touring urban areas or hipster locations, or going to Japan to examine new ways of packaging products, bringing the "outside in" is a powerful source of creative inspiration.

  Bringing in cultural extremes (e.g., tattoo artists, musicians, and authors) will also bring new inspiration to innovation.

- Trending and Macro Forces: Taking the long view, by combining several converging trends, will help develop a future state for a category. Then, create a new three- to five-year innovation plan within which transformational opportunities can be developed.

- Blog Surfing: The web can be tricky, especially in these times where there can be a fair amount of disinformation and posturing. That said, using blogs and blog-like information can be really helpful to reveal meaningful insights about brands, products, and categories.

  Many teams have started here. Several years ago, I think this would have made a good starting point for new ideas. Now I would suggest this as useful data to triangulate with other data sources.

Hands-on

- Prototype the Idea: Prototyping's chief purpose is to give the ideas structure.

  Once you know the problems end users want to solve, co-create the prototypes with the end users. They can be expressed as a drawing, storyboard, web site, or an app. They can be more three-dimensional by creating prototypes from spare parts. New Product Ventures, a design firm in Connecticut, develops workshops where they create customer prototypes in 3D printers—later bringing them back to their customer designers for review and modification.

  From all of this, you get physical thought-starters grounded in the needs of your users.

- Product Test: This is where fast feedback loops are essential and allow you to excel at rapid prototyping. Bring in potential users from your target audience and walk them through the prototypes, simulate usage, and then gather feedback.

12. Expressing and Testing Your Idea

Expressing the product idea as a concept for testing is the next step. The concept is the customer-facing expression of the idea that distills it into a tightly articulated package of clear benefits and reasons to purchase. Think of concepts as the luggage for your idea. They make the idea portable so that you can take it anywhere and show it to anyone.

The concept is similar to brand positioning in that everything you need to know to build the concept is already known. A well-written concept enables you to verify that the attributes and benefits of the idea are meaningful to your customer target.

Your concept should:

- Have a product name
- Be grounded in the insight revealed from your work
- Speak the benefit of the idea
- Provide support as to why your product can deliver
- Cover product particulars such as flavor, pricing, etc.

Concept Validation

Methods for concept validation come in all shapes and sizes, depending on the industry.

When it comes to CPG, marketers have relied on AC Nielsen's BASES tests for decades as the gold standard. BASES use data from over 200,000 global tests across sixty-eight markets to help marketers measure the interest in new products, their features, and their benefits.[56]

BASES include in its survey work a series of factors that it has correlated with successful product launches. It compares those results to its database to predict volume and revenue. If there is a marketing plan, it factors in the spending to refine the estimates.

BASES has three levels to its testing based on how finished the product is and whether or not a marketing plan is available.

Other companies deploy different types of studies that range from simplified purchase interest models to the highly complex choice model studies that model attribute and benefit trade-offs and their impact on purchase interest.

TEST

What is most important is that you test. Don't launch a product without some level of valid testing with an end-user or target customer.

It is easy to discount research if the product idea or concept doesn't test well. Be thoughtful. Instead, look at the data and see why the product concept failed. Then make improvements to the idea so that it doesn't. It is common (and tempting) to believe your idea delivers on all of the key requirements even when most ideas don't. You have to be honest with yourself and open to hearing what customers say... even when it's not what you want to hear.

This is why we test—to mitigate the downside and optimize for maximum return.

13. Closing Thoughts on Growth, Innovation, and M&A

People do find ways to be incredibly successful by getting lucky and having all the planets align to create something from nothing. It is in our nature to be hopeful to think that the next new idea will make it. But, lightning doesn't strike often. Most new products fail. More often than not, start-ups fail.

Success comes from disciplined approaches to understanding the marketplace, trends, and customer needs, and then applying solid strategic thinking on how to roll out those ideas.

Bonus Chapter

"People will forget what you said, people will forget what you did, but people will never forget how you made them feel."
—Maya Angelou

CHAPTER 12

Profit with Honor

2004

L ike most of us, I've worked for some really great people and some really awful people. The CEO and CMO at Big Heart Pet Brands were among the best. They developed their people, stayed open minded, mentored them and groomed them for personal growth. I feel fortunate to have had the chance to work for them.

For every good one there is a least two bad ones. One, that I will never forget, kept a bowl of little plastic monkeys on his desk. If you gave him a deck he didn't like or wanted you to change, he would give you a plastic monkey. If you said something he did not like, he would give you a plastic monkey. He wouldn't take the monkey back till you did exactly what he wanted to his satisfaction. This was literally "getting the monkey off your back." Not so great.

2014

I've always been a players' coach. I knew the challenges that my teams were been going through. There were rumors in the halls that there was going to be a buyout, and no one knew what that meant. Mostly, it meant uncertainty. The team was worried about their jobs.

Our team had really jelled into a fantastic group of marketing research and insights consultants in a large CPG company. We were well respected. Our partners in the organization asked for our advice, even if they weren't asking for new research. But, now the team morale was down.

In the long run, I knew that the buyout was going to work to most everyone's benefit, but there was only so much I could share at this early time. I needed a collective distraction. So, I made up one.

I created the purple ball game. The rules of the game:

- Each member of the team would get a soft purple ball.
- It would be their job to decorate that purple ball in any fashion they wished.
- The only two rules were that:
  - They couldn't "hurt" the ball. The ball has feelings. The purple ball was a homunculus—an artificially made, miniature person or creature.
  - Team members were not allowed to identify whose ball was whose.
- During the two weeks, the purple balls were moved around the office, to desks, doorknobs, and communal spaces. This way, everyone saw all of the purple balls, and playful pranks were fair game.
- At the end of two weeks, we had a team lunch, culminating with a purple ball celebration.

The purple ball game required minimal effort and time on anyone's part. It built team morale and deflected the negative energy away from the tension created by the buyout. And, I believe, it brought the team closer.

1. My Journey

Writing this book has been cathartic. My journey and my stories flooded back into memory. There have been so many people, so many brands, so many categories, and so many challenges—good, bad and funny. I never mentioned:

- The client who yelled at me for not divulging the anonymous respondent names from a survey we conducted for him, so that he could add them to his sales sheet to contact.
- The Kibbles 'N Bits commercial shoot, where the script called for the actors to eat at the family table. There were so many takes that they had to chew and spit out their food over and over again just so they wouldn't get sick.
- Playing SEGA video games to work on their branding and new products. Having fun and building a brand and category.
- Playing broom hockey in MACRO Consulting's two-room office with the only other person in the fledgling company. Having fun and making no money.
- Creating a segmentation and new algorithms that would turn around an entire phone business go-to market.
- Pulling countless all-nighters analyzing data and preparing presentations.
- Or, one of my favorites, traveling around Brazil looking for new fruits to bring to the U.S.—meeting amazing people and becoming immersed in an amazing culture.

As I reflected on my own experiences, I realized that most of the challenges, successes, and failures that we run into, as marketers and as market researchers, start with interpersonal relationships.

2. It Doesn't Matter Who's Right

I've always counseled my teams that it doesn't matter where the great idea comes from. What matters is that the great idea happens. Meaning that listening to each other, building upon each other's ideas, and not being wed to your idea merely because you thought of it, is fundamental to making sure the great ideas happen and championed.

"Checking your ego at the door" is fundamental to bringing ideas to life—you must have an openness to everyone's point of view. I know it's hard when you are convinced you are right and that you have all the answers.

But, teamwork matters. Selfless support matters. Shared goals matter. Winning together actually does matter. Sometimes, though, it takes a willingness to let others lead and be right.

Market researchers, because they have access to the data and insights, always think they know all that they need to know. The marketer, on the other hand, knows what is needed to accomplish objectives, goals, strategies, tactics, and metrics. With that clear vision, brand marketers may see a straight line between themselves and the objective.

Just like the researcher needs to understand the marketer, the marketer needs to understand the researcher. They don't always have to agree. Tension is okay. Conflict is not.

3. Getting Out of the Box

Showing each other respect is crucial to achieving shared success. The book *Leadership and Self Deception* from the Arbinger Institute illustrates how to think about working relationships and how every person comes to the table with their own challenges.[57]

Loosely speaking, the book addresses how you approach your relationship with colleagues. You may already have formed an opinion about them or their agenda even before you've met them. In your mind, you've placed them in a metaphorical box. That box that you've created for them does not let them be anything else other than what you decided they are (this happens in all aspects of society.)

Instead, you need to allow yourself to get to know the entire person. Try to understand what might be going on in their role, what might be going on in other meetings, and what might be going on with that person outside of work.

All those things are a reason for getting out of the box. It becomes so easy to criticize what others are doing when you have already formed an opinion of them. It is much harder to be accepting and understanding when you realize there is more to a person than meets the eye.

4. Personal Impact

> *"Just think if you can have an impact here,*
> *how big that will be."*
> —Jim Nyce, the Head of Pepsi Insights

I always felt that PepsiCo was too big to effect change. It is a gigantic company. How can you affect change in such a big company? The analog would be a large ship. Big boats move slowly. Jim and I talked about that, and he reminded me that small changes could turn into significant changes.

To that end, you start to realize that your potential for impact includes:

- Your organization's goals
- Your team's success
- The individuals whom you support
- The individuals who support you, and the people who support them

It gets granular quickly. You are in service of all those people. If you make one person feel better at work, they go home, and maybe they feel better when they're at home.

Your impact reaches more people than you think.

5. Principles

The word authenticity is tossed around quite a bit these days. The Greek word *authentikos* can be translated as "genuine." Authenticity means your actions are genuine and consistent with your beliefs and values.

I've tried to be genuine both professionally and personally. So, when I say there are a set of principles that are worthy of your consideration, I hope you will take them to heart. It has taken a career to arrive at them, and I believe that they work.

- Your word is the creation of your integrity. Negative results come from negative actions. Everything you are is illustrated by your actions.
  - o Don't treat others with arrogance
  - o If you lie, you will lose trust.
  - o If you treat someone poorly, you will lose trust—with that person as well as with everyone else who observes that action.
  - o Simply, when you act negatively, bad things will come from it.

- Reflect on what is important. Too often, people can get caught up in the stress of the day—worrying about what decisions are being made, and what management is doing.
  - o At work and in life, focus on the things that matter.
  - o Only focus on what you can control.
  - o Have a genuine concern for the welfare of others.

- Choose partners wisely—the company you keep and the conversations you have with them is essential. Don't be part of that group that gossips or talks behind the backs of others. Just walk away from that conversation. Gossip is counterproductive.
  - o Avoid useless talk.
  - o Refuse the morbid fascination with other people's problems.

6. Keep an Open Mind

I like to think I've kept an open mind to new and sometimes entirely different ways of working over the years. I'd recommend:

- Bringing mindfulness and heartfulness to the team.
- Adding meditation to your training.
- Blocking out a conference room for quiet time, so that individuals can get away from the noise of public spaces.
- Vision boarding to encourage individuals to work toward their personal life goals—no matter where they would be. If someone's vision is not consistent with where they are at that moment, help that person get to where they want to be.
- Adding conflict management and resolution role-playing to understand the challenges of others. Role-playing may not be revolutionary, but it is incredibly valuable to work on listening skills, teamwork, and understanding others.
- Annual full team off-sites. Semi-annual leadership offsites.

7. Lifelong Learning

There are many brilliant quotes, talks, articles, blogs, and books on leadership philosophy. I will add only this to the long list of leadership prescriptions:

- Be a lifelong learner. Don't assume you know everything. Listen and learn. When you get feedback—that you didn't expect—view it as a gift. Mentor and be mentored. Find more than one person who can reverse mentor you so that you can continue to learn from multiple viewpoints. Like great ideas, learning can come from anywhere and anybody.

8. Manifestations

One of the more important business books I have read is the *Diamond Cutter – The Buddha on Managing Your Business and Your Life.*[58] It is not an easy read. But, my key takeaways come in the chapter entitled, "The Correlations of Common Business Problems and Their Solutions." This chapter made the whole book worthwhile.

Here are a few of the principal manifestations that I think are the most important:

- To prosper financially, be generous. Even if your business is down, find ways to reward your team.
- To see yourself in a world that is happy, maintain an ethical way of life.
- To focus your mind, practice meditation.
- To get all you wished for, practice compassion toward others.
- To see yourself as a leader, take joy in constructive and helpful actions.

9. Our World: Do Better Than Do No Harm

I was having a conversation with a member of my team who had moved on to a new company. She was (and is) a star, developing and maturing as a person and a leader every day.

However, she was troubled. She had found that the corporations she had worked for were not "walking the talk" where the environment and sustainability were concerned. In her mind, companies will spend time doing what they can within their power to improve upon their environmental footprint as long as it works within the P&L and meets shareholder objectives.

Acquisitions can be driven by the need to move the parent company into a more favorable light with the customer and to adopt more sustainable practices. It helps them attract talent and meet the higher-order needs of the customer.

I applaud all these actions—small steps matter. The integrity of your word matters, even though it may be difficult. Keep pushing the ball forward. Don't always opt-out for value engineering by swapping high-quality ingredients for something of lesser quality to capture more profits. Your customers will recognize what you've done and either reward you for staying the course or walk away from you for having caved.

Instead, be in the game for the long haul. Leave a positive legacy. Your customers will be loyal, advocate for you, and be customers for life.

Thank you!

If you have gotten this far in this book, I am grateful for your time. I care about these things, about getting it right, about insight-driven marketing strategy, about listening, and about working together toward shared goals and great achievements.

End Notes

[1] https://en.wikipedia.org/wiki/Product/market_fit, March, 2020

[2] Schneider, Joan and Julie Hall. "Why Most Product Launches Fail." Harvard Business Review. April 2011. Accessible at: https://hbr.org/2011/04/why-most-product-launches-fail. Accessed April 21, 2020.

[3] Accessible at: https://www.wired.com/2013/08/remembering-the-apple-newtons-prophetic-failure-and-lasting-ideals/ Accessed April 21, 2020

[4] "Global Market Research 2018." ESOMAR. 22 September 2018. ISBN: 92-831-0302-5. Available at: https://www.esomar.org/knowledge-center/library/Global-Market-Research-2018-pub2898. Accessed April 21, 2020.

[5] "When Corporate Innovation Goes Bad — The 160 Biggest Product Failures of All Time." CB Insights. 7 April June 2020. Available at: https://www.cbinsights.com/research/corporate-innovation-product-fails/. Accessed 7 May 2020.

[6] Berg, Chip. "The CEO of Levi Strauss on Leading an Iconic Brand Back to Growth." Harvard Business Review. 01 July 2018.

[7] Strauss, William and Neil Howe (1991). Generations. Ft. Mill, SC: Quill House Publishing.

[8] Brown, Anna. "Younger men play video games, but so do a diverse group of other Americans." Pew Research Center. 11 September 2017. Accessible at: https://www.pewresearch.org/fact-tank/2017/09/11/younger-men-play-video-games-but-so-do-a-diverse-group-of-other-americans/. Accessed 7 May 2020.

[9] Sitzmann, T. (2011), A Meta-Analytic Examination of the Instructional Effectiveness of Computer-based Simulation Games. Personnel Psychology, 64: 489-528. doi:10.1111/j.1744-6570.2011.01190.x

[10] Occulus Web site: https://www.oculus.com/

[11] Uber: Arrington, Michael. "What If UberCab Pulls An Airbnb? Taxi Business Could (Finally) Get Some Disruption?" TechCrunch. 31 August 2010.

Accessed at: https://techcrunch.com/2010/08/31/what-if-ubercab-pulls-an-airbnb-taxi-business-could-finally-get-some-disruption/

Lyft: Primack, Dan. "Why Ubers CEO was Right to Kneepcap Lyft." Fortune. 11 November 2014. Accessed at: https://fortune.com/2014/11/11/why-ubers-ceo-was-right-to-kneecap-lyfts-fundraising/. Accessed on 15 April 2020.

[12] Arrington, Michael. "What If UberCab Pulls An Airbnb? Taxi Business Could (Finally) Get Some Disruption." TechCrunch. 31 August 2010. Accessible at: https://techcrunch.com/2010/08/31/what-if-ubercab-pulls-an-airbnb-taxi-business-could-finally-get-some-disruption/?guccounter=1. Last Accessed: 7 May 2020.

[13] Rodionova, Zlata. "Uber and Airbnb only used by the young, rich and well-educated, study finds A third of US adults have never even heard of Uber." The Independent. 19 May 2016. Accessible at: https://www.independent.co.uk/news/business/news/uber-and-airbnb-are-only-used-by-the-young-rich-and-well-educated-study-finds-a7037531.html. Last Accessed 7 May 2020.

[14] Primack, Dan. "Why Uber was right to 'kneecap' Lyft's fundraising." Fortune. 11 November 2014. Accessible at: https://fortune.com/2014/11/11/why-ubers-ceo-was-right-to-kneecap-lyfts-fundraising/. Last accessed: 7 May 2020.

[15] Issac, Mike. "What You Need to Know About #DeleteUber." The New York Times. 31 January 2017. Accessible at: https://www.nytimes.com/2017/01/31/business/delete-uber.html. Last accessed: 7 May 2020.

[16] Fry, Richard. "Millennials projected to overtake Baby Boomers as America's largest generation." Pew Research Center. 1 March 2018.

[17] Brager, Danny. "Generations on Tap: Beverage Alcohol Purchases Vary By Age Group." Nielsen Insights. 11 August 2014. Accessible at: https://www.nielsen.com/us/en/insights/article/2014/generations-on-tap-beverage-alcohol-purchases-vary-by-age-group/. Accessed 7 May 2020.

[18] Fry, Richard. "Millennials projected to overtake Baby Boomers as America's largest generation." Pew Research Center. 1 March 2018. See: https://www.pewresearch.org/fact-tank/2018/03/01/millennials-overtake-baby-s/

[19] Dimock, Michael. "Defining generations: Where Millennials end and Generation Z begins." Pew Research Center. 17 January 2019.

[20] "Spending Habits by Generation." US Department of Labor. 3 November 2016. Accessed at: https://blog.dol.gov/2016/11/03/spending-habits-by-generation. Last Accessed 7 May 2020.

[21] "Gains in Translation: What Your Language Choices Say to US Hispanics." Facebook IQ. 4 October 2016. Accessible at: https://www.facebook.com/business/news/insights/gains-in-translation-what-your-language-choices-say-to-us-hispanicsAccessed: 15 April 2020.

[22] Dimock, Michael, et. Al. "Political Polarization in the American Public." Pew Research Center. 12 June 2014, Page 13. Accessible at: https://www.people-press.org/2014/06/12/political-polarization-in-the-american-public/. Accessed 7 May 2020.

[23] "Mission Statement: Starbucks Coffee Company." Starbuck Web site. Accessible at: https://www.starbucks.com/about-us/company-information/mission-statement. Accessed on 15 April 2020.

"DelMonte Foods Becomes Big Heart Pet Brands." Pet Business. 20 February 2014. Accessible at: http://www.petbusiness.com/February-2014/Del-Monte-Foods-Becomes-Big-Heart-Pet-Brands/. Accessed on 15 April 2020.

"Our Mission." Nike Web site. 20 February 2014. Accessible at: https://about.nike.com/. Accessed on 15 April 2020.

Schleckser Jim. "Apple's Boring Mission Statement and what we can learn from it." Inc. 16 August 2016. Accessible at: https://www.inc.com/jim-schleckser/apple-s-boring-mission-statement-and-what-we-can-learn-from-it.html. Accessed on 15 April 2020.

"Amy's Kitchen, Inc." http://about.spud.com/portfolio-item/amys-kitchen-inc/ 19 March 2014. Accessed on 15 April 2020.

"Warby Parker History." Warby Parker Web site. Accessible at: https://www.warbyparker.com/history. 15 April 2020. Accessed on 15 April 2020.

"About Tesla." Tesla Corporate Web site: https://www.tesla.com/about?redirect=no. 15 April 2020. Accessed on 15 April 2020.

"How Personalisation Can Help You Connect to Your Customers in a Whole New Way."

[24] "Kikoko Company Web site." https://kikoko.com/. Accessed on 15 April 2020.

[25] (RED) Manifesto: "(RED) AIDS Awareness Campaign." Accessible at: https://redaidsawareness.weebly.com/red-manifesto.html. Accessed on 15 April 2020.

Levi's Go Forth: "Levi's "Go Forth" Legacy Campaign Manifesto." Accessible at: https://www.pinterest.com/pin/243124079854008634/. Accessed on 15 April 2020.

Apple: "Think Different." Accessible at: https://adage.com/creativity/work/think-different-manifesto/24719. Accessed on 15 April 2020.

[26] "Definition of Strategy." Lexico (powered by Oxford). Accessible at: https://www.lexico.com/en/definition/strategy. Accessed on 15 April 2020.

[27] Clarke. Molly. "57 Essential Multichannel Marketing Statistics." ZoomInfo. Accessed at: https://blog.zoominfo.com/multichannel-marketing-statistics/. Accessed 7 May 2020.

[28] US Digital Ad Spending Will Surpass Traditional in 2019." Emarketer. 19 February 2019.

[29] Story, Louise. "Anywhere the Eye Can See, It's Likely to See an Ad." The New York Times. 15 January 2007.

[30] Kruger, Alyson. "When Mom Slams a Brand on Instagram." The New York Times. 26 November 2019. Accessible at: https://www.nytimes.com/2019/11/26/business/mommy-influencers.html. Accessed 7 May 2020.

[31] Cheskin, Louis. (2016). Color for Profit. New York: Rebel Books.

[32] "Most Americans Say That the Design of a Product's Packaging Often Influences Their Purchase Decisions." Press Release: Ipsos. Accessible at: https://www.ipsos.com/en-us/news-polls/Most-Americans-Say-That-the-Design-of-a-Products-Packaging-Often-Influences-Their-Purchase-Decisions. Accessed on 15 April 2020.

33 "What to Do when There Are Too Many Product Choices on the Store Shelves?" Consumer Reports. January 2014. Accessible at: https://www.consumerreports.org/cro/magazine/2014/03/too-many-product-choices-in-supermarkets/index.htm. Accessed on: 7 May 2020.

34 "Individual Snacking Categories On The Rise in The U.S." Nielsen Insights. 22 November 2017. Accessible at: https://www.nielsen.com/us/en/insights/article/2017/individual-snacking-categories-on-the-rise-in-the-us/. Last Accessed: 7 May 2020.

35 "What to Learn From Tropicana's Packaging Redesign Failure?" Marion – The Branding Journal. May, 2015.

36 Gonzalez, Guadalupe. "How Uber's IPO Stacks Up Against the Most Highly Anticipated tech IPOs in History." Inc. Magazine. 9 May 2019.

37 Anderson, Chris (2004). Long Tail: Why the Future of Business Is Selling Less of More. New York, NY: Writers of the Round Table Press.

38 Catmull, Ed and Amy Wallace (2014). "Creativity, Inc.: Overcoming the Unseen Forces That Stand in the Way of True Inspiration." New York, NY: Random House.

39 "Biopharmaceutical Research & Development." Pharmaceutical Researches and Manufacturing Association. Accessible at: http://phrma-docs.phrma.org/sites/default/files/pdf/rd_brochure_022307.pdf. Last Accessed 7 May 2020.

40 Cheng, Andrea. "CPG Giants, Desperate For Growth, Seek Out Once-Unthinkable Tie-Ups And Push M&A To 15-Year High." Forbes. 10 July 2018.

41 Sutherland, Jeff and Deena Shanker. "Kellogg Sells Keebler, Snacks to Ferrero for $1.3 Billion." Fortune. 1 April 2019.

42 Dahl, Brian. "Brand Strategy: Branded House vs. House of Brands." DKY. 31 May 2016. Accessible at: https://dkyinc.com/2016/05/building-a-winning-brand-strategy-brand-hierarchy. Accessed 15 April 2020.

43 O'Reilly, Lara. "Why it doesn't matter if people think 'Alphabet' is a good brand name or not." Business Insider. 11 August 2015.

[44] "Branded House or House of Brands?" Ideasbig.com. 21 July 2016. Accessible at: https://www.ideasbig.com/blog/branded-house-house-brands/. Accessed 15 April 2020.

[45] Neal Hansch@nhansch (2016). "Why the top entrepreneurs are seeking corporate venture money." TechCrunch. 11 October 2016.

[46] "How tech Leaders Navigated Crisis & Crossroads: Microsoft, Apple, Slack & More." CBInsights. Accessible at: https://www.cbinsights.com/research/report/business-tech-memos-lessons/. Accessed 15 April 2020.

[47] Brunet, Sebastien Brunet, et. Al. "Global Accelerator Report 2016." Gust.com. Accessible at: http://gust.com/accelerator_reports/2016/global/. Last Accessed on: 7 May 2020.

[48] "About Us." Kitchentown.com. Accessible at: https://kitchentowncentral.com/about-us/. Last Accessed 7 May 2020.

[49] "339 Start-up Failure Post Mortems." CBInsights. Accessible at: https://www.cbinsights.com/research/start-up-failure-post-mortem/ Last Accessed 7 May 2020.

[50] "State of Innovation Report." CBInsights. Accessible at: https://www.cbinsights.com/research-state-of-innovation-report. Last Accessed 7 May 2020.

[51] Hoffman, Reid and Ben Casnocha (2012). The Start-up of You. New York: Random House.

[52] "The Top 20 Reasons Start-ups Fail." CBInsights. Accessible at: https://www.cbinsights.com/research/start-up-failure-reasons-top/. Last Accessed 7 May 2020.

[53] Team, Trefis. "Here's How Valuable The Wearables Business Is To Nike." Forbes. 23 May 2014. Accessible at: https://www.forbes.com/sites/greatspeculations/2014/05/23/heres-how-valuable-the-wearables-business-is-to-nike/. Last Accessed 7 May 2020.

[54] "What Is Dropbox?" Accessible at: https://www.dropbox.com/features/. Accessed 15 April 2020.

[55] "Design Thinking." IDEO U. Accessible at: https://www.ideou.com/pages/design-thinking. Last Accessed 15 April 2012

[56] "Innovate for Growth." Neilsen. Accessible at: https://www.nielsen.com/us/en/solutions/product-development/. Last Accessed 15 April 2012

[57] "Leadership and Self Deception" (2018). New York, NY: Berrett-Koehler Publishers.

[58] Roach. Geshe (2000). "The Diamond Cutter: The Buddha on Strategies for Managing Your Business and Your Life" (2000). New York: Doubleday.

Acknowledgments

Writing a book is just not as easy as I thought it would be. Everything in this book comes from years of experience with friends, colleagues, and frenemies. There's just too many to list—people from Delaware Valley Meats, ARBOR, Bruzzone, Dataquest, Cheskin+Masten, MACRO, Copernicus, PepsiCo, Del Monte, Big Heart Pet Brands, KitchenTown, and all of my clients. All of the people who have worked for me and all of the people for whom I have worked.

Special thanks to my friends and family for their support; to David Krawlik, who kept me on track; to Kathy Oneto for her keen editing eye; to Dick McCullough for his never-ending insults; to Pop; to the G4; to Joy for absolutely everything; and to Zach for his help and inspiration.

Author's Bio

Jonathan Weiner has been working in Marketing Strategy for over thirty-five years. Born out of his love for market research and understanding the customer, he has always been a champion of customer-first strategy.

He was the SVP of Marketing Services, Strategy and Customer Experience at Big Heart Pet Brands; the Vice President of Strategy and Insights at Del Monte; and the Director of Strategy & Insights at PepsiCo. Prior to founding JW Consulting and Advisory, he was the Chief Marketing Officer at the global food incubator Kitchentown.

In his consulting career, Jonathan worked in a wide range of B2C and B2B categories and for some of the largest brands in the world, including Apple, Google, and Levi Strauss.

He has led and run seminars on marketing excellence, spoken at conferences on marketing and insights, and guest-lectured for the American Marketing Association, Yale, and Haas Business Schools.

He has been working with Patagonia Actionworks in conjunction with Catchafire to support nonprofits that need assistance with marketing and marketing strategy.

He currently lives in the San Francisco Bay Area, running JW Consulting and Advisory, and is an investor and start-up advisor.

www.ingramcontent.com/pod-product-compliance
Lightning Source LLC
Chambersburg PA
CBHW022035190326
41520CB00008B/588